CREOLE-ENGLISH
ENGLISH-CREOLE
DICTIONARY

T0275393

HIPPOCRENE CONCISE DICTIONARY

CREOLE-ENGLISH
ENGLISH-CREOLE

Charmant Theodore

HIPPOCRENE BOOKS
New York

For information, address:
HIPPOCRENE BOOKS, INC.
171 Madison Avenue
New York, NY 10016

ISBN-13: 978-0-7818-0275-8
ISBN-10: 0-7818-0275-X

Printed in the United States of America.

CONTENTS

CREOLE-ENGLISH

A

abandone [abahndona] *v* abandon
abdike [abdikeh] *v* abdicate
abese [abehseh] *v* debase, lower
abèy [abehy] *n* bee
abi [abee] *n* abuse
abilite [abiliteh] *n* ability
abitan [abeetanh] *n* peasant
abitid [abeeteed] *n* habit
abitye [abityeh] *adj* used to, coping
abiye [ahbeeyeh] *v* clothe, dress
abiyman, rad garment
abize [abeezeh] *v* abuse
abjèk [abject] *adj* abject
aboli [ahbolee] *v* abolish
abondan [abonhdanh] *adj* abundant,
  bountiful, profuse
abòne [abohneh] *v* subscribe
abreje [abrhajeh] *v* abbreviate
abriko [abreeko] *adj* amber, *n* apricot
abrip [ahbreep] *adj* steep
absans [ahbsanhs] *n* absence
absid [abseed] *adj* absurd

absòbe   [apsohbeh] *v* absorb
absoud   [ahbsout] *v* absolve
abstrenn   [abstrenh] *v* abstain
acha   [ashah] *n* purchase
acheval   [ashehvahl] *adj* captious
achte   [ashteh] *v* buy
adapte   [adahpteh] *v* adapt
adekwa   [adehkwah] *adj* adequate
adikte   [adikteh] *adv* addict
adilt   [adeelt] *n* adult
adistans   [ahdistanhs] *adj* far, remote
adisyone   [adeesioneh] *v* add
adjektif   [adjecteef] *n* adjective
admèt   [admayt] *v* admit
admiratè   [admeerateh] *n* admirer
admire   [admeereh] *v* admire
adolesan   [adohlesanh] *n* adolescent
adopte   [adohpteh] *v* adopt
adore   [adohreh] adore
adrès   [adrayhs] *n* address
afab   [afahb] *adj* amiable, bland
afè   [afayh] *n* affair, bargain, business
afekte   [afekteh] *v* affect
afere   [afehreh] *adj* busy
afiche   [afeeshay] *v* affix
afime   [afeemeh] *v* affirm

afron [afronh] *n* affront
afronte [afronhteh] *v* affront
agase [ahgahseh] *v* enrage
agraf [agraph] *n* clasp
ajamè [ahjahmeh] *adv* forever
ajan [ahjanh] *n* money, silver; agent
aje [ahjeh] *adj* old; elder, senior
aji [ajee] *v* act
ajil [ajeel] *adj* lest, agile, nimble; deft *n*
  clay
ajiste [ajeesteh] *v* adjust
ajou [ahjoo] *adj* up-to-date
ajoune [ajouhneh] *v* adjourn
ajoute [ajouhteh] *v* add
ak [ahk] *conj* and; with
akeri [akehree] *v* acquire, gain
akimile [akimileh] *v* accumulate, gather
akite [akeeteh] *v* acquit
akize [akeezeh] *v* accuse, indict
aklè [ahkleh] *adj* evident
akò [akohr] *n* agreement, accord
akò [akohr] *n* agreement, covenant
akòde [akohrdeh] *v* accord
akomode [akomodeh] *v* accommodate
akonpli [akonhplee] *v* accomplish, execute,
  perform

akoste [akosteh] *v* accost

akote [akohteh] *adv* aside, beside, near

akouchman [akooshmanh] *n* labor, giving birth

akouple [ahkoopleh] breed, mate

akòz [akoz] *conj* because

aks [acks] *n* axis; axe

aksè [akseh] *n* access

aksede [aksehdeh] *v* accede

aksepte [aksepteh] *v* accept

aksidan [akseedanh] *n* accident

aksidantèl [aksidantayl] *adj* casual

aksyon [aksionh] *n* action, deed

aksyonen [actionenh] *v* actuate

alame [alameh] *v* alram, scare

alantou [alanhtou] *adv* around

ale [aleh] *v* go; *n* alley

ale pou vini [alepoovini] *adv* vice-versa

aleche [alehsheh] *v* lure

aleka [alaykah] *adj* detached

alèkile [alehkeeleh] *adv* nowadays, presently

alemye [ahlehmyeh] *n* relief, improvement, betterment

alèn [aleihn] *n* breath

alimante [ahleemanhteh] *v* feed; power

alimèt [aleemet] *n* match

aliyen [ahleeyenh] *v* align
alizyon [aleezionh] *n* allusion
alò [aloh] *prp* so
altere [altereh] *v* alter, change
alyaj [aleeaj] *n* compound
alye [alieh] *n* ally
amalgame [amhlgahmeh] *v* merge
amann [ahman] *n* fine
amatè [amahteh] *n* amateur
amati [amatee] *n* casing
ame [ameh] *v* arm, *n* army
amelyore [amehlioreh] *v* improve
amenajman [amenahjmanh] *n* amenity;
   comfort, setting
amensi [ahmensee] *v* reduce
amizan [ameezanh] *adj* fun, amusing,
   pleasant
amize [ameezae] *v* amuse, entertain
amizman [ameezmanh] *n* fun
amòti [mohtee] *v* deaden, damper
anana [ahnahna] *n* pineapple
anba [anhbah] *prep* below, beneath,
   underneath, bottom, under
anbachal [anhbashal] *adj* illicit, covert
anbake [anhbakeh] *v* embark, board
anbale [anhbahleh] *v* bundle, pack

12

anbarase [anhbaraseh] *adj* embarrassed, perplex

anbasad [anhbasad] *n* embassy

anbasadè [anhbasadeh] *n* ambassador

anbatè [anhbateh] *n* underground

anbativant [anhbateevanht] *n* stomach

anbeli [anhbelee] *v* embellish, *n* clearing

anbete [anhbehtae] *v* bother

anbouteyaj [anhbooteyaj] *n* jam

anbrase [anhbraseh] *v* hug, kiss

andedan [anhdehdanh] *prp* in

andedan [anhdedanh] *n* inside

andedan [anhdedanh] *adv* inside, within

andeyò [anhdeyoh] *n* countryside, province

andeyò [anhdeyoh] *adj* external, *adv* out

andikape [anhdikapae] *adj* handicapped; disabled

andirans [anhdeeranhs] *n* endurance

andòmi [anhdohmee] *adj* sleepy, sedate

ane [ahneh] *n* year

anfle [anhfleh] *adj* swollen, *v* swell

anfòm [anhfom] *adj* fine, elegant

angaje [anhgaje] *adj* involved

angl [anhgl] *n* angle

angle [anhgleh] *adj* English

anile [ahnilae] *v* annihilate, cancel

animal   [aneemal] *n* animal
animatè   [aneemateh] *n* animator, host
anime   [aneemeh] *adj* brisk
ankadreman   [anhkadrehmanh] *n* frame
ankiloze   [anhkeelozeh] *adj* numb, dull
ankò   [anhkohr] *adv* again, anew
ankonbre   [anhkonhbreh] *v* overcrowd
ankonbre   [anhkonhbray] *adj* crowded
ankouraje   [anhkourajeh] *v* encourage, urge
anksyete   [anxsieteh] *n* anxiety
anlè   [anhlay] *prep* above, atop, up, over
anlè   [anhlayh] *n* surface, top
anlve   [ahnlveh] *v* abduct, kidnap
anmè   [anhmeh] *adj* bitter
anmèdan   [anhmehdanh] *adj* disturbing
anmède   [anhmehdae] *v* disturb, bother
anmède   [anhmehdeh] *v* annoy, peeve
annavans   [anavahns] *adv* early
anniye   [anhniyeh] *adj* bored, annoyed, *v*
   annoy
annò   [annoh] *adj* golden
anonse   [ahnonhseh] *v* announce
anouvo   [ahnouvoh] *adv* anew, afresh
anpakte   [anhpakteh] *v* pack
anpeche   [anhpesheh] *v* impeach, deter; stop
anpenpan   [anhpenhpanh] *adj* elegant, fine

anpil   [anhpeel] *adj* much, many; most; very
anplwaye   [anhplwayeh] *v* employ
anpoche   [anhposheh] *v* pocket
anpremye   [anhprehmyeh] *adj* first, primary
anpren   [anhprenh] *n* loan
anprèsman   [anhpressmanh] *n* haste, zeal
anpwazonnen   [anhpwazonhnenh] *v* poison
anreta   [anhreta] *adv* late
anrichi   [anhrishee] *v* enrich
anrole   [anhwoleh] *v* draft, recruit
anroule   [anhrooleh] *v* loop
ansanm   [anhsanhm] *adj* together, *adv* along
ansante   [anhsanteh] *adj* healthy
ansèk   [anhsek] *adj* circular
ansekirite   [anhsehkiriteh] *adj* secure
ansèkle   [anhsehkleh] *v* surround
ansent   [anhsent] *adj* expectant, pregnant;
   with child
anseye   [anhsehyeh] *v* teach
ansibreka   [anhseebrehkah] *adj* uneven,
   flimsy, rickety
ansòsele   [anhsohsle] *v* bewitch
ansyen   [anhsyenh] *adj* ancient, old
ant   [anht] *prep* between
antèman   [anhtehmanh] *n* funeral, burial
antere   [anhtereh] *v* bury

15

antèt [anhteht] *n* heading

antete [antehteh] *adj* determined, head strong

antouzyas [anhtoozyas] *adj* enthusiastic, rapt

antravè [anhtraveh] *adv* athwart

antre [anhtreh] *n* entrance, door, *v* enter

antren [anhtrenh] *n* zest

antrepriz [anhtrehpriz] *n* enterprise, venture

antye [anhtyeh] *adj* whole,

anvayi [anhvayee] *v* invade; flood

anverite [anhveriteh] *adv* quite

anvi [anhvee] *v* desire, crave *n* envy, birth mark

anviron [anhveeronh] *adv* around, nearly

anvlòp [anhvlohp] *n/v* envelop

anvye [anvyeh] *v* envy, *adj* envious

anyen [anhyenh] *prp* nothing

apa [apah] *adj* separate, *n* lure (fishing)

apante [ahpanhteh] *v* survey, pace

apèl [apehl] *n* roll call; appeal (court)

apendis [apenhdis] *n* appendix

apik [ahpeek] *adj* elevated, high

apiye [ahpeeyeh] *v* lean

aplodi [aplohdi] *v* cheer

aprann [ahpran] *v* learn

apre   [apreh] *prep* after
apresye   [apresyeh] *v* appreciate
aproche   [aprosheh] *v* approach
apropo   [apwopo] *prp* about
apropriye   [apwopriyeh] *adj* appropriate
aprouve   [apwouhve] *v* approve
aptitud   [aptiteed] *n* ability
apwen   [ahpwenh] *adj* ripe
apwofondi   [aprofondih] *adj* careful
apye   [apyeh] *adv* afoot
ar   [ahr] *n* art
aran   [ahranh] *n* herring
arestasyon   [arestasionh] *n* arrest
arete   [areteh] *v* arrest, apprehend
arete   [arehteh] *v* arrest, detain
arid   [ahreed] *adj* arid, infertile
arid   [ahrid] *adj* arid
arogan   [arohganh] *adj* arrogant
arondi   [awonhdee] *v* round
aroze   [ahrohze] *v* water, baste
aryenafè   [aryenhnafeh] *adj* idle, joker
asasen   [asahsenh] *n* murderer, killer
asayi   [ahsayee] *v* attack, assail
ase   [ahseh] *adv* enough, *adj* sufficient,
   ample, enough
ase   [ahseh] *adv* enough; quite

asezonman [asehzonhmanh] *n* seasoning, relish

asfalt [asfalt] *n* asphalt

asfalt [asfahlt] *n* asphalt; pavement

asire [ahseereh] *v* assure, insure, *adj* confident

asiste [ahsisteh] *v* attend, assist

aspè [aspeh] *n* aspect, angle

aswè [asweh] *n* tonight

asye [asyeh] *n* steel

asyeje [ahsyejeh] *v* besiege

asyèt [asyeht] *n* dish, plate

atach [atash] *n* brace

atak [ahtak] *n* attack, raid

atake [ahtakeh] *v* attack

atansyon [atanhsionh] *inter* watch out!

atansyon [atanhsionh] *n* attention, *inter* Attention!

atantif [atanhtif] *adj* attentive

atenn [atennh], *v* arrive, attain, reach

ateste [ahtesteh] *v* attest

ateste [ahtesteh] *v* attest *v*

atifisyèl [ahtifisiehl] *adj* artificial, bogus, false

atik [atik] *n* article

atire [ahtireh] *v* attract

atitud [ahtiteed] *n* attitude, mood
atmosfè [atmosfè] *n* ambiance
atoufè [atoofeh] *adj/n* desperate
atrap [ahtrap] *v* catch, grasp
atravè [atraveh] *adv* across
atròs [atwos] *adj* atrocious
atroupman [atroopmanh] *n* gathering, riot
avalide [avalihdeh] *v* avouch
avalwa [avalwa] *n* advance
avan [avanh] *prp* before
avanjou [avanhjoo] *n* dawn
avans [avanhs] *n* advance
avanse [avanhseh] *v* move forward, promote
avantaj [avanhtaj] *n* advantage
avèg [avhegh] *adj* blind
avegle [avegleh] *v* blind, dazzle
avèk [avek] *prp* with
avèti [avehtee] notify
avèti [avehtee] *v* warn
avi [avee] *n* notice, *adv* for life
avni [avnee] *n* future
avnu [avnue] *n* avenue
avoka [avohka] *n* attorney, lawyer
avril [avreel] *n* April
avwan [avwahn] *n* oat
awoze [awohzeh] *v* water, irrigate

ayisyen [ahyeesyenh] *adj* Haitian
ayisyèn [ahyeesyehn] *adj* Haitian (fem.)
azil [azeel] *n* asylum

B

ba   [bah] *adj* low, *n* stocking
bab panyòl   [babpanhyol] *n* moss
bab   [bab] *n* beard
babako   [babako] *n* feast; barbeque
babote   [baboteh] *v* dabble
bachote   [bashoteh] *v* cram
bag   [bag] *n* ring
bagay   [baguy] *n* thing, something, object
bagay   [bahgahy] *n* object, thing
bal   [bahl] *n* bullet; bale; packet
balans   [bahlanhs] *n* equilibrium; balance,
    scale
balanse   [balanhseh] *v* actuate, swing, rock
balansin   [balanseen] *n* swing
bale   [baleh] *n/v* broom, *v* sweep
balèn   [bahlehn] *n* whale
balon   [balonh] *n* ball
bambòch   [banhbosh] *n* feast
ban   [banh] *n* bench
banal   [bahnahl] *adj* ordinary
bande   [banhdeh] *v* band, wrap; *adj* horny
bani   [banee] *v* banish

bankal   [bankal] *adj* bent, crooked, warped
bankè   [bankeh] *n* banquet
bankèt   [banhket] *n* bench
bann   [ban] *n* flock, group; erection
banyè   [banyeh] *n* banner
baraj   [baraj] *n* dam
bare   [bahreh] *v* obstruct, block
bare   [bahreh] *v* block, catch, capture, corner
baro   [bahro] *n* rail
baryè   [bahryeh] *n* gate, fence
basen   [basenh] *n* basin, pond
askètbòl   [basketball] *n* basketball
baskile   [baskeeleh] *v* flip
bat   [bat] *v* hit, defeat
batay   [batie] *n* battle, scuffle
batay   [bahtie] *n/v* fight, quarrel
batèm   [batehm] *n* baptism
bati   [batee] *v* build
batiman   [bateemunh] *n* boat
bato   [batoe] *n* boat, ship
baton   [batonh] *n* baton, rod, stick
batri   [batree] *n* battery
bay   [bye] *v* give, procure
bay koutba   [bye kootba] *v* deceive
bay   [bye] *v* give
bay kouraj   [bye kooraj] *v* embolden

bay gabèl   [bye gahbel] *v* dare
bay bourad   [bye boorad] *v* boost, push
baye   [bayeh] *v* yawn
baylegen   [byelegenh] *v* surrender, give up
baz   [baz] *n* base, foundation
bè   [beh] *n* butter
bebe   [beh-beh] *n* baby
bèbè   [behbeh] *adj* mute
bèf   [behf] *n* bull, ox
bege   [begey] *v* stutter, stammer
begle   [beglay] *v* bellow
beke   [bekeh] *v* peck, *n* try
bekonn   [baykon] *n* bacon
bèl   [bell] *adj* pretty, handsome; cute
bèlantre   [behlantreh] *adv* welcome
bèlfi   [belfee] *n* daughter-in-law
bèlte   [behlteh] *n* charm, beauty
benediksyon   [benedikseeonh] *n* blessing
benefis   [benefis] *n* benefit
benefisye   [behnehfeesyeh] *v* benefit, enjoy
benefisyèl   [benefisyel] *adj* beneficial
benevòl   [benevol] *adj* benevolent
beny   [benhye] *n* bath
benyen   [benhyenh] *v* bathe
berè   [bereh] *n* cap
bese   [behseh] *v* lower, decline

bèso [behso] *n* cradle
bèt [beht] *n* animal, beast *adj* imbecile, daft
bèt [beht] *v* ridicule
etay [behtie] *n* cattle
bètkay [behtkye] *n* pet
bètrav [behtrahve] *n* beet
bezwen [behzwenh] *n/v* need
bileng [beeleng] *adj* bilingual
bilten [billtenh] *n* bulletin; ballot
bis [bis] *n* bus
bisiklèt [beeseeklet] *n* bicycle
bistro [beestro] *n* pub
bit tè [beet teh] *n* clod
bivèt [beevet] *n* banquet
biwo [beewo] *n* desk, office
blabla [blabla] *v* blab
blag [blahg] *n* joke
blam [blam] *n* blame
blame [blahmeh] *v* blame
blan [blanh] *adj* white; blank
blanchi [blanhchee] *v* bleach
blayi [blajyee] *v* spread
ble [bleh] *adj* blue, azure
ble [bleh] *n* wheat
blese [blehseh] *n/v* wound, cut
blesi [blehsee] *n* wound, cut

24

bliye [bleeyeh] *v* forget
blòf [bluff] *n* bluff
blofe [blofeh] *v* bluff
blòk [block] *n* block, chump
bloke [blokeh] *v* block, *adj* congest
bo [bo] *n/v* kiss
bò [boh] *n* brim; side
bobin [bohbeen] *n* reel
bobine [bohbeeneh] *v* reel
bòde [bohrdeh] *v* accost; trim
bòdi [bohdee] *n* border, contour, hedge; trim
bòdmè [bodmeh] *n* seashore
bofis [bohfis] *n* son-in-law
bokal [bohkal] *n* jar
bòl [bol] *n* bowl
bon [bonh] *adj* good
bon gou [bongoo] *adj* delicious
bon mache [bonmasheh] *adj* cheap
bòn [bonn] *n* maid, servant
bonbe [bonhbay] *v* bulge
bonbon [bonhbonh] *n* cake; candy
Bondye [bonhdyeh] *n* God
bonè [bohneh] *adv* early
bònfwa [bohnfwa] *n* good faith, earnest
bonm [bonm] *n* bomb; pan
bòs [boss] *n* foreman

bòt [boot] *n* boot
bouch [boosh] *n* mouth
bouche [boosheh] *v* block, stop, *adj* congested
bouche [boosheh] *v* plug; enclose
bouche [boosheh] *v* obstruct, stop
bouche [boosheh] *n* butcher
bouchon [booshonh] *n* cap, lid
bouchon lyèj [booshonh leehej] *n* cork
boujon [boojonh] *n* bud
bouk [book] *n* village
boukannen [bookanenh] *v* roast
boukè [boukeh] *n* bouquet
boul [bool] *n* ball; lie
boul [bool] *n* ball
boule [booleh] *n/v* burn
boulon [boolonh] *n* bolt; nut; screw
bounda [bounda] *n* ass, behind
boure [booreh] *v* stuff, cram; saturate
bourik [boorik] *n* donkey, ass
bous [boos] *n* purse, wallet
bouskilad [booskeelad] *n* rush
boustabak [boostabak] *n* crow, raven
bout [boot] *n* end, limit, edge
bout kanson [boot kanhsonh] *n* short
boutbwa [bootbwa] *n* log

26

boutèy [bootehy] *n* bottle
boutik [bootik] *n* store, shop
bouton [bootonh] *n* button; pimple
boutonnen [bootonenh] *v* button
bouya [booya] *n* fog
bouyay [booyay] *n* trouble, disorder
bouyi [booyee] *v* boil *adj* boiled
bouyon [booyonh] *n* broth, stew
bouyon [booyonh] *n* broth, minestrone
bra [brha] *n* arm
brak [brak] *adj* acrid, tart
branch [brahnsh] *n* limb, bough
branche [bransheh] *v* connect
branlan [branhlanh] *adj* loose, flimsy, shaky, precarious
brase [brahseh] *v* stir
brav [brav] *adj* brave, courageous
braye [brayeh] *v* bawl
brèf [brehf] *adj* concise, short
bretèl [bretehl] *n* brace, suspenders
bri [bree] *n* noise, rumor
bridsoukou [breedsookoo] *adj* abrupt
brik [brick] *n* brick
bripbrip [bripbrip] *adj* abrupt
brital [breetal] *adj* brutal, rough, *n* brute
briyan [breeyanh] *adj* bright

27

briz [breeze] *n* breeze
brize [breezay] *v* break
brode [brodeh] *v* embroider, knit
bròs [bwos] *n* brush
brose [bwoseh] *v* brush
bwa [bwa] *n* wood, lumber
bwa chapant [bwa shapant] *n* timber
bwat [bwat] *n* box, case
bwatchèn [bwatshen] *n* oak
bwè [bweh] *v* drink
bweson [bwesonh] *n* drink
bwote [bwoteh] *v* haul
byè [byeh] *n* beer, ale
byen tonbe [byentonhbeh] *adj* fitting,
    suitable
byen [beeyenh] *n* wealth, property, fortune,
    adv well
yenfezans [bienhfehzanhs] *n* beneficence
byennere [byenehreh] *adj* blissful
byennèt [byenet] *n* welfare

CH

chabon   [shabonh] *n* coal, charcoal
chagren   [shagrenh] *n* chagrin, grief, regret, sorrow
chaj   [shaj] *n* charge, load
chaje   [shahjeh] *v* load, charge
chak   [shak] *adj* each
chalimo   [shalimo] *n* straw
cham   [sham] *n* charm, beauty; appeal
chame   [sahmeh] *v* charm, bewitch
chamo   [shamo] *n* camel
chandèl   [shandel] *n* candle
chandelye   [shandeleeheh] *n* chandelier
chanje   [shanjeh] *v* change, shift; switch
chanm   [shanhm] *n* bedroom, chamber, room
chanpiyon   [shanhpiyonh] *n* mushroom
chanpyon   [shanpeeonh] *n* champion
chans   [shans] *n* chance, luck
chante   [shanteh] *v* sing, *n* song
chape   [shahpeh] *v* survive
chapit   [shahpit] *n* chapter
chapo   [shahpo] *n* hat
charite   [shahriteh] *n* charity

charony [sharonhy] *n* carrion, decay
charyo [shareeo] *n* cart, carriage
chase [shahseh] *v* chase, evict
chat [shat] *n* cat, kitten
chato [shato] *n* castle
chè [sheh] *adj* expensive; precious, *n* flesh
chèche [shehsheh] *v* look for, fetch, search, seek
chèf [chef] *n* chief
chèk [shek] *n* cheque
chekè [shaker] n checker
chèlbè [shelbeh] *adj* vain, fancy
chemen [shehmenh] *n* road, route, way
chemine [chemineh] *n* chimney
chemiz [shemiz] *n* shirt
chen [shenh] *n* dog
chenn [shen] *n* chain
cheri [sheri] *n/adj* dear, darling
chèsè [shehseh] *n* nun
cheval [chehval] *n* horse
cheve [shehveh] *n* hair
chèz [shez] *n* chair, seat
chif [shif] *n* digit, number
chiklèt [sheklet] *n* chewing gum
chirijyen [shereejienh] *n* surgeon
chita [shetah] *n* sit

cho   [show] *adj* hot, excited
chode   [shodeh] *v* scald
chofe   [shofeh] *v* heat up, *adj* hot, heated
chofè   [shofeuh] *n* driver, chauffeur
chòk   [shock] *n* bump, shock
choke   [shokeh] *v* shock
chosèt   [shoset] *n* sock
chòt   [shot] *n* short
chou   [shoe] *n* cabbage
chòv   [shove] *adj* bald
chòvsourit   [shove sourit] *n* bat
chuichui   [shwishwi] *n* rumor *v* whisper
chwa   [shwah] *n* choice
chwal   [shwal] *n* horse
chwazi   [chwazi] *v* choose, elect, select

D

dakò   [dakoh] *v* agree, *n* in agreement
dan   [danh] *n* tooth
danje   [danhje] *n* danger, peril
danre   [danhreh] *n* goods, produce
dans   [danhs] *n* dance
danse   [dahnseh] *v* dance
dantis   [danhtis] *n* dentist
dapiyan   [dapeeyanh] *v* grab, ravish
dayè   [dayeh] *prp* besides
dayiva   [diver] *n* diver
de   [deh] *adj* two
debarase   [dehbaraseh] *v* rid
debarase   [debaraseh] *v* clear, unblock
debat   [dehbat] *v* debate, deliberate
debat   [dehbat] *v* debate
debòch   [debosh] *n* debauch
debòde   [dehbodeh] *v* overflow
debouse   [dehbouseh] *v* disburse
debouya   [debouyah] *adj* diligent, nifty
debouye   [debouyeh] *v* cope, manage
dechikte   [dehshikteh] *v* jag *adj* ragged
dechire   [dehsheereh] *v* tear

dechouke [deshookeh] *v* depose, uproot

deden [dehdenh] *n* disdain

defann [dehfan] *v* prohibit,forbid; defend

defans [dehfans] *n* defense

defayans [defayanhs] *n* lapse, deterioration

defè [dehfeh] *v* undo

definitif [definitif] *adj* definite

defo fabrik [dehfofabrik] *n* defect

defo [defo] *n* default

defòme [defomeh] *v* distort

defwa [dehfwa] *adv* twice

defye [dehfyeh] *v* pini, defy; dare

degi [dehgee] *adj* additional

degou [dehgoo] *n* disgust

degoutan [dehgootanh] *adj* lousy,
    disgusting, nasty

degoutan [dehgoutanh] *adj* disgusting,
    abject

degoute [dehgooteh] *v* drip, disgust

degre [dehgreh] *n* degree, diploma

deja [dehja] *adv* already, yet

dejne [dejneh] *n* breakfast

dekadans [dekadenhs] *n* decadence

deklare [dehklareh] *v* declare, affirm, state

dekont [dehkont] *n* count

dekore   [dehkoreh] *v* decorate

dekouraje   [dehkoorajeh] *v* discourage

dekouvri   [dekoovree] *v* discover, discern

dekrè   [dehkreh] *n* decree

dekri   [dehkree] *v* describe

delala   [dehlala] *adj* delirious

deli   [deleej] *n* deluge, inundation

elika   [dehlika] *adj* delicate

delivre   [deleevreh] *v* deliver

delye   [dehlyhe] *v* dilute

demach   [dehmash] *n* project; gait

demanjezon   [dehmanhjehzonh] *n* itch

demann   [dehman] *n* demand

demanti   [dehmanhtee] *v* belie

demantle   [dehmanhtleh] *v* raze

demen   [dehmenh] *n* tomorrow

demi   [dehmee] *adj* half

demode   [dehmohdeh] *adj* outdated, obsolete

demoli   [dehmolee] *v* demolish

demon   [dehmonh] *n* devil

demontre   [dehmontreh] *v* demonstrate,
   depict

demoralize   [demohralizeh] *v* demoralize

dènye   [dehnyeh] *adj* last

depa   [dehpa] *n* departure

depann   [dehpan] *v* depend, trust

depans [dehpanhs] *n* expense

depanse [dehpanhseh] *v* spend

depase [dehpaseh] *v* exceed, overcome, surpass

depatman [dehpatmanh] *n* department, county

depi [dehpee] *adv* ago, since

deplase [dehplaseh] *v* displace, move

deplimen [dehpleemenh] *v* pluck

depo [dehpo] *n* depot, deposit

deposede [dehposehdeh] *v* dispossess, disown

depòte [dehpohteh] *v* deport

depoze [dehpozeh] *v* deposit, put

deranje [dehranhjeh] *v* annoy, molest, intrude

deranje [dehranjeh] *v* disturb, disable, *adj* disabled

derechany [dehrehshanhy] *n* spare

desanm [dehsanm] *n* December

desann [dehsanh] *v* descend, to go down

desann [desann] *v* camp, stay

desè [dehseh] *n* dessert

desen [desenh] *n* design

desepsyon [dehsepseeonh] *n* deception

desevwa [dehsehvwa] *v* disappoint, deceive

deside   [dehseedeh] *v* decide

desizyon   [dehseezeeonh] *n* decision, judgement, verdict

destine   [destineh] *n* destiny

destine   [destineh] *n* fate

dèt   [det] *n* debt

detache   [dehtacheh] *v* detach

detache   [dehtacheh] *adj* apart, *v* separate

detann   [dehtan] *v* relax

detekte   [dehtekteh] *v* detect

detèmine   [dehtehmineh] *adj* determined

deteste   [dehtesteh] *v* detest, hate

detonasyon   [dehtonaseeonh] *n* detonation, bang

detou   [dehtoo] *n* detour

detounen   [dehtoonenh] *v* deprave; hijack

detounen   [dehtoonenh] *v* avert, avoid

detwi   [dehtwi] *v* destroy

devalize   [dehvahleezeh] *v* ransack

devan   [dehvanh] *n* front

devan   [dehvan] *v* advance! forward!

devan   [dehvanh] *adj/prp* ahead

devanjou   [dehvanhjoo] *n* dawn

devaste   [dehvasteh] *v* devastate, ravage

devide   [dehveedeh] *v* spill

devine   [dehveeneh] *v* guess

devinèt [dehveenet] *n* riddle, puzzle
devlope [dehvlopeh] *v* develop
devwale [dehvwaleh] *v* unravel, reveal
devwe [dehvweh] *adj* devout
devyasyon [dehviahseeonh] *n* deviation
dèyè [dehyeh] *n* buttock, *prep* behind, after
dèyè [dehyeh] *n* behind; ass
deyò [dehyo] *adj* out, illegitimate
deyò [dehyoh] *n* outside
dezabiye [dehzabeeheh] *v* undress
dezagreyab [dehzagreyab] *adj* desagreable
dezagreyab [dezagreab] *adj* disagreable
dezakò [dezakoh] *n* discord
dezaprouve [dezaprooveh] *v* disapprove
dezas [dezas] *n* disaster
dezavantaj [dezavanhtaj] *n* disadvantage, drawback
dezè [dezeh] *n* desert
dezenvòlt [desinhvohlt] *adj* casual
dezespere [dezespereh] *v* despair *adj* desperate
deziyen [dazeeyenh] *v* appoint
deziyen [dehziyenh] *v* assign
dezobeyi [dezohbehyee] *v* disobey, violate
dezòd [dehzod] *n* mess
dezòd [dehzod] *n* disorder

37

dezonè   [dehzohneh] *n* shame
dezonè   [dehzoneh] *n* dishonor, disgrace
dezoryante   [dehzorianteh] *v* bewilder
dezyèm   [dehzyem] [*adj* second
dezyèm men   [dezyem menh] *adj* used,
   second hand
di   [dee] *adj* callous, hard, harsh; strong
di   [dee] *v* say
dife   [deefeh] *n* fire
diferan   [difehranh] *adj* different
difisil   [difisil] *adj* difficult
dijere   [deejereh] *v* digest
diksyonè   [dikseeoneh] *n* dictionary
dimanch   [deemansh] *n* Sunday
dimansyon   [deemansyonh] *n* dimension,
   size
diminye   [dimineeheh] *v* decrease, diminish;
   abase
dine   [deeneh] *n* dinner, *v* dine
diplome   [deeplomeh] *adj/v* graduate
dirèk   [deerek] *adj* direct, *n* director
direksyon   [deereksyonh] *n* direction
direktè   [deerekteh] n director, chairperson,
   manager
diri   [deeree] *n* rice
dirije   [deereejeh] *v* lead, command, direct

dis [dees] *adj* ten

diskisyon [diskeeseeonh] *n* discussion, brawl

diskite [diskeeteh] *v* discuss, debate

diskite [dikeeteh] *v* discuss

diskrè [diskreh] *adj* discrete

diskresyon [diskrehseeonh] *n* discretion

dispansè [dispanhseh] *n* dispensary

disparèt [deesparet] *v* vanish

disparèt [disparet] *v* disappear

disparèt [dispahret] *v* disappear, fade

disponib [disponib] *adj* available

distans [distanhs] *n* distance

disten [distenh] *adj* distinct

distenge [distenhgeh] *v* distinguish, *adj* distinguished

distrè [distreh] *v* distract, *adj* disturbed

distri [distree] *n* district

distribye [deestribyeh] *v* distribute

diton [deetonh] *n* proverb

divage [deevageh] *v* ramble

diven [deevenh] *n* wine

divès [deeves] *adj* various

divès [deeves] *adj* diverse

divize [divizeh] *v* divide

divòs [deevos] *n/v* divorce

diyite   [deeyiteh] *n* dignity
diznèf   [deeznef] *adj* nineteen
dizuit   [deezuit] *adj* eighteen
djal   [jall] *n* girl
djin   [djeen] *n* gin; jeans
djipsi   [gypsy] *n* Gypsy
djòb   [job] *n* job, work
djògin   [jogging]*n* jogging
djòl   [jol] *n* snout
djòlè   [djohleh] *adj* boastful
djòlè   [djohleh] *n* show off
djondjon   [jonhjonh] *n* mushroom
dlo   [dloh] *n* water; stream, river
dodin   [dodeen] *n* rocking chair
dodinen   [dodeenenh] *v* rock
dokazyon   [dokazyon] *adj* used
dokiman   [dokeemanh] *n* document, file
dola   [dola] *n* dollar
dòlote   [dolloteh] *v* pamper, coddle
domaj   [domaj] *n* damage
domaje   [domajeh] *v* damage
dòmi   [domee] *v* sleep
domine   [dohmeeneh] *v* dominate, prevail
don   [donh] *n* gift, talent
done   [dohneh] *n* data, given
donnen   [donnhenh] *v* yield

donte [donhteh] *v* tame
dosye [doseeheh] *n* file, brief
dosye [dosyeh] *n* record, file
dòtwa [dohtwa] *n* dormitory
dou [do] *adj* sweet, mellow
doub [doob] *adj* double
double [doobleh] *v* double
douch [douche] *n* shower
doulè [dooleh] *n* pain, pang
doulè [dewleh] *n* ache, pain
dous [doos] *adj* sweet; sleej, *n* sweets
dousman [doosmanh] *adv* slowly; *adj* slow, quiet
dout [doot] *n* doubt
doute [dooteh] *v* doubt
douz [dooz] *adj* twelve
dra [dra] *n* linen, cover, sheet
drapo [drapoh] *n* flag
drese [drehseh] *v* rear, tame; erect, raise
dròg [dwog] *n* drug
droge [dwogeh] *adj* addict, drugged, *v* drug
dròl [dwol] *adj* odd, funny, strange
droum [dwoom] *n* drum
dwa [ladwann] *n* fee
dwa [dwah] *n* right; law
dwat [dwat] *adj* straight; right

dwe   [dweh] *v* owe
dwèt   [dwet] *n* finger

E

e   [eh] *conj* {how, what} about
eblouyi   [eblooyi] *v* dazzle; amaze
echanj   [eshanhj] *n* exchange, trade, swap
echantiyon   [eshanhteeyonh] *n* sample
echap   [ehshap] *n* sling
echèk   [eshek] *n* chess
èd   [aid] *n* aid, support
ede   [ehdeh] *v* help, assist
edike   [edeekeh] *v* educate
edite   [edeeteh] *v* edit
efarouche   [efawoosheh] *v* apall, scare
efase   [efaseh] *v* delete, erase, efface
efò   [ehfoh] *n* effort
efreyan   [ehfrehyanh] *adj* frightening,
   hideous
efreye   [ehfrehyeh] *v* scare
egal   [ehgal] *adj* equal, even,
egare   [egareh] *adj* gaga, confused
egi   [ehgee] *n* needle
egou   [ehgoo] *n* drain
egoyis   [ehgoyis] *adj* selfish
egzajere   [egzajehreh] *v* exaggerate

egzak [exak] *adj* exact

egzamen [egzamenh] *n* exam, test, quiz

egzamine [egzameeneh] *v* examine, view

egzan [egzanh] *adj* exempt

egzanp [egzanp] *n* example

egzanplè [egzanpleh] *n* sample, *adj* exemplar

egzekite [egzeketeh] *v* execute, perform

egzèsis [egzehsis] *n* drill, exercise

egzistans [existanhs] *n* existence

egziste [egzeesteh] *v* exist

ekip [ehkeep] *n* team

ekip [ekeep] *n* crew, team

ekipe [ekeepeh[*v* equip, furnish

ekipman [ekeepmanh] *n* equipment

ekla [ehklah] *n* glitter, glare

eklate [ehklateh] *v* explode

eklate [eklateh] *v* explode, burst, erupt

eklatman [eklatmanh] *n* explosion, eruption

eklere [ehklereh] *adj* intelligent, bright

eklèsi [eklehsi] *v* clarify, *n* clearing

eko [ehko] *n* echo

ekòs [ekos] *n* bark

ekran [ehkranh] *n* screen

ekri [ehkree] *v* write, correspond

ekriven [ehkreevenh] *n* writer, author

eksede   [eksehdeh] *v* exceed
eksepsyon   [eksepsyonh] *n* exception
eksepte   [eksepteh] *adj* except
eksite   [ekseeteh] *v* excite, abet, arouse
ekspè   [ekspeh] *n* expert
eksperyans   [eksperyanhs] *n* experience
eksplike   [expleekeh] *v* explain
eksplisit   [ekspleeseet] *adj* explicit
eksplore   [e(k)splohreh] *v* explore
eksploze   [e(k)splohzeh] *v* explode
eksplozyon   [e(k)splozyonh] *n* explosion
ekspòtasyon   [e(k)spotasyonh] *n* export
ekspòte   [e(k)spoteh] *v* export
ekspoze   [e(k)spozeh] *v* expose
ekspozisyon   [e(k)spozeesyonh] *n* exposition
eksprime   [e(k)spreemeh] *v* express
eksteryè   [ekstehryeh] *n* exterior
ekstraòdinè   [e(k)straohdeeneh] *adj*
   extraordinary
ekstrè   [e(k)streh] *n/v* extract; *n* digest
ekstrèm   [e(k)strem] *adj* extreme
ekzòbitan   [ekzobitanh] *adj* exorbitant,
   outrageous
elabore   [ehlaboreht] *v* elaborate
elaji   [ehlajee] *v* expand, enlarge
elefan   [ehlehfanh] *n* elephant

eleksyon   [ehleksyonh] *n* election, poll
elèv   [ehlev] *n* pupil
eli   [ehlee] *v* elect
elimine   [ehleemeeneh] *v* eliminate
elòj   [ehlohj] *n* compliment
elòj   [ehloj] *n* praise
elve   [ehlveh] *v* rear
emab   [aymab] *adj* amiable, bland
emèt   [emet] *v* emit
emèt   [ehmet] *v* emit
emisyon   [emeesyonh] *n* broadcast
emosyon   [ehmosyonh] *n* emotion
en   [enh] *adj* one
èn   [ehn] *n* hatred
enbesil   [enhbehseel] *adj* fool, imbecile, silly
enbesil   [enhbesil] *adj* imbecile, dumb
endiferan   [enhdiferanh] *adj* indifferent,
   distant; aloof
endijan   [enhdeejanh] *n* indigent, pauper
endike   [enhdeekeh] *v* indicate
endiyasyon   [enhdeeyasyonh] *n* indignation
enève   [ehneveh] *v* enrage, *adj* tense,
   nervous
enfekte   [enhfekteh] *v* infect
enfim   [enhfim] *adj* crippled, disabled,
   handicapped

enfimyè [enhfeemyeh] *n* nurse
enfliyans [enhfleeyanhs] *n* influence
enigm [enigm] *n* enigma
enkapab [enhkapab] *adj* incapable,
  inadequate, unable
enklinasyon [enhklinehzonh] *n* inclination
enkomode [enhkomodeh] *v* incommodate
enkonsyan [enhkonhsyanh] *adj* oblivious,
  careless
enkwayab [enhkwayab] *adj* incredible
enkyetid [enhkietid] *n* worry, anxiety
enòm [ehnom] *adj* enormous
enpas [enhpass] *n* deadlock
enpasyan [enhpasyanh] *adj* impatient
enpe [enhpeh] *adj* some, a few; a little
enplije [enhpleekeh] *v* implicate
enplore [enhploreh] *v* implore, plead
enplwaye [anhplwayeh] *v* hire; use
enposib [enhpohsib] *adj* impossible
enpòtan [enhpotanh] *adj* important,
  imposing
enpresyone [enhpresyoneh] *v* impress
enpridan [enhpreedanh] *adj* imprudent, rash
enprime [enhpreemeh] *v* print
ensèk [enhsek] *n* bug, insect
ensilt [enhsilt] *n* insult

ensipòtab [enhseepotab] *adj* unbearable
ensiste [enhseesteh] *v* insist
ensite [enhsiteh] *v* abet, incite
enskri [enhskree] *v* record
ensolan [enhsolanh] *adj* insolent
enstantane [enhstanhtaneh] *adj*
 instantaneous
enstige [ensteegeh] *v* entice
enstriman [enhstrimanh] *n* instrument, tool
entansyon [enhtanhsyonh] *n* intention,
 purpose
entèdi [enhtehdi] *v* prohibit, ban
entèdiksyon [enhtediksyonh] *n* prohibition
entèfere [enhtehfehreh] *v* interfere
entelijan [enhtelijanh] *adj* clever,
 intelligent,
entelijans [entelijanhs] *n* intelligence, wit
enterese [enhtereseh] *adj* interested, eager
entèronp [enhteronhp] *v* interrupt
entimide [enhtimideh] *v* intimidate, daunt
entrige [enhtreegeh] *v* intrigue, fascinate
envante [enhvanhteh] *v* invent
envite [enhveeteh] *n* guest, *v* invite
envizib [enhveezeeb] *adj* invisible
envoke [enhvokeh] *v* invoke,
epè [epeh] *adj* thick, fat

epè [epeh] *adj* dense, thick
epi [ehpee] *conj* then
erè [ehreh] *n* error
erè [ehreh] *n* error
eritaj [ehreetaj] *n* inheritance
esans [ehsanhs] *n* extract
esè [ehseh] *n* try, attempt
eseye [ehsehyeh] *v* try
eskalye [eskahlyeh] *n* stair
eskiz [eskeez[*n* excuse
eskize [eskeezeh] *v* excuse
eskòte [eskoteh] *v* escort
espas [espahs] *n* space
espase [espahseh] *v* space
espere [espehreh] *v* hope
espesaylman [espesyalmanh] *adj* especially
espesyal [espesyal] *adj* especial, particular
esprè [esprey] *adj* deliberate
espresyon [esprehsyonh] *n* expression, utterance
espri [espree] *n* spirit
espyonaj [espionage] *n* espionage
estim [esteem] *n* esteem
estime [esteemeh] *v* appraise, estimate
estipid [esteepeed] *adj* stupid

estraòdinè   [estraodeeneh] *adj*
  extraordinary, uncommon
estropye   [estwopyeh] *v* cripple
etabli   [etahblee] *v* establish, *adj* settled
etajè   [etahjeh] *n* rack, shelf
etalaj   [ehtalaj] *n* array, display
etale   [ehtaleh] *v* display, spread
etanda   [ehtandah] *n* stand
etann   [ehtan] *v* extend, open
etann   [ehtann] *v* expand
etap   [ehtap] *n* stage
ete   [ehteh] *n* summer
etenn   [ehten] *v* turn off, quench, *adj* off
etènye   [ehtenyeh] *v* sneeze
etidye   [ehteedyeh] *v* study
etonan   [ehtonanh] *adj* amazing
etone   [ehtoneh] *v* surprise, wonder, *adj*
  surprised
etranje   [ehtranhjeh] *adj* strange, *n* alien,
  stranger
anje   [ehtranhjeh] *adj* foreign, *n* foreigner
etwal   [etwal] *n* star
etwat   [etwat] *adj* narrow
evade   [ehvahdeh] *v* evade, break out (jail)
evalue   [ehvalueh] *v* estimate, appraise
evalyasyon   [ehvalyasyonh] *n* evaluation

evalye [evahlyeh] *v* evaluate
evalye [ehvahlyeh] *v* evaluate, estimate
evenman [ehvehnmanh] *n* event, surprise
evidan [ehveedanh] *adj* evident, obvious
evite [ehveeteh] *v* avoid, avert, prevent
ezitan [ehzitanh] *adj* hesitating
ezite [ehzeeteh] *v* hesitate

F

fab   [fab] *n* detergent; fable
fabrik   [fabreek] *n* factory
fabrike   [fabreekeh] *v* make, build,
  manufacture
fache   [fasheh] *adj* angry, *v* trouble, upset
faktè   [fakteh] *n* postman
falèz   [falez] *n* cliff
familyarize   [familiareezeh] *v* accustom,
  familiarize
familye   [familieh] *adj* familiar, colloquial
famin   [fameen] *n* dearth, famine
fanatik   [fanatik] *adj* fan, fond; bigot
fanm   [fahnm] *n* woman
fanmi   [fanhmee] *n* family, relative
fann   [fhan] *v* split, cleave
fant   [fanht] *n* slit, crack, gap
fantom   [fanhtom] *n* ghost, phantom
farin   [farin] *n* flour
farinen   [fareenenh] *v* drizzle
fasil   [fahseel] *adj* easy
fasine   [fahseeneh] *v* fascinate
fatig   [fateeg] *n* fatigue

fatigan [fahteegan] *adj* tiring, tedious, trying

fatige [fahteegeh] *v* tire

fatra [fahtrah] *n* trash, mess, refuse

favè [fahveh] *n* favor

favorab [favorab] *adj* favorable, auspicious

favorize [favoreezeh] *v* favor, condone

fayit [faheet] *n* doom, failure; deficit

fè pati [fehpatee] *v* belong, participate

fè [feh] *v* do, build, make

fè reklam [feh rayklam] *v* publicize, boost

fè egzèsis [fehegzesis] *v* exercise, exert

fè konpliman [feh konhpleemanh] *v* congratulate

fè demann [fehdeman] *v* inquire

fè sote [fehsoteh] *v* startle; astound

fè jouda [fehjooda] *v* peep, snoop

fè djòlè [fehjoleh] *v* bawl

è konfyans [fehkonhfyans] *v* trust

fè jwenn [feh jwen] *v* procure, facilitate

fè bab [fehbab] *v* shave

fè payas [fehpahyass] *v* connive

fè konesans [fehkonesanhs] *v* acquaint *v*

fè pitit [feh piteet] *v* procreate

fè atansyon [fahtanhsyonh] *v* heed

fè [feh] *n* iron

fèb [fehb] *adj* weak, bleak, feeble
fèjedou [fehjedoo] *v* wink
fèm [fehm] *n* farm, *adj* solid, firm
femèl [fehmel] *adj* female
femèl chen [fehmelchenh] *n* bitch
fèmen [fehmenh] *v* close; enclose, shut, *adj* locked, shut
fen [fen] *adj* fine, keen, thin, *n* end, aftermath
fen [fenh] *adj* fine, thin
fenèt [fehnet] *n* window
fennen [fenhnenh] *v* fade, wither, shrivel
fente [fent] *n* simulation
fènwa [fehnwa] *adj* obscure
fern [fèurn] foujè
feròs [fehros] *adj* ferocious
fèsiyo [fehseeyo] *v* signal, wink
fèt [feht] *n* party, anniversary
fevriye [fehvreeyeh] *n* February
fèy [fhey] *n* leaf
fi [fee] *n* female, woman, girl
figi [feegee] *n* face
figire [feegeereh] *v* calculate
fiks [fix] *adj* steady
fikse [fiksey] *v* stare, gaze; scrutinize
fiksyon [fiksyonh] *n* fiction

fil (elektrik)   [feelehlektreek] *n* wire
fil (akoud)   [feelakood] *n* thread
fil (arenyen)   [feelarenhyenh] *n* cobweb
filange   [feelanhgeh] *v* chop, mince
file   [feeleh] *v* court, flirt; whet *adj* sharp
fimen   [feemenh] *v* smoke
fimye   [feemyeh] *n* dung, muck
final   [feenal] *adj* final
fineray   [feenehrahy] *n* funeral
fini   [feenee] *v* finish
firye   [feeryeh] *adj* furious
fisèl   [feesel] *n* string
fizi   [feezee] *n* rifle
fizye   [feezyeh] *v* shoot
flanbe   [flanhmbay] *v* blaze, flare
flanke deyò   [flanhke deyoh] *v* chuck, kick
   out
flanm   [flanhm] *n* blaze, flame
flannen   [flanhnenh] *v* drift, rove, stray,
   wander
flè mayi   [flehmahee] *n* cornflower
flè   [fleh] n flower, blossom
flèch   [flesh] *n* arrow, dart
flechi   [fleshy] *v* flinch
fleri   [flehree] *v* flower, bloom
flèsolèy   [flehsoley] *n* sunflower

flote [flotay] *v* drift, float

fo [fo] *adj* false, bogus

fò [foh] *adj* strong, brilliant, intelligent

fò [foh] *adj* loud

fobou [fohboo] *n* suburb

fòje [fojeh] *adj* wrought; made up

fòm [fom] *n* shape

fòmann [forman] *n* foreman

fòme [fomeh] *v* form, machine; *adj* matured

fon [fonh] *adj* deep, profound, *n* bottom

fondasyon [fonhdahsyonh] *n* foundation, base

fonn [fun] *v* melt, merge

fonse [fonhsay] *v* leap, *adj* dark

forè [fohreh] *n* forest

fòs [foss] *n* strength, courage

fòs [foss] *n* force, effort

fòse [fohseh] *v* force, strain, *adj* compelled

fòt [fot] *n* fault, mistake

fotèy [fohtaye] *n* armchair, sofa

fòtin [foteen] *n* fortune, wealth

foto [photo] *n* photo

fou [foo] *n* oven

fou [foo] *adj* crazy, delirious, insane

fouchèt [fooshet] *n* fork

foul [fool] *adj* loaded, full, crowded

56

foumi   [foomee] *n* ant

founen   [foonenh] *v* bake, *n* batch

founi   [foonee] *v* cater, provide, supply

founi   [foonee] *adj* furnished

foure   [fooreh] *v* insert

foure   [fooreh] *v* engage

fouye   [fooyeh] *v* dig, delve

frajil   [frajeel] *adj* fragile, sensitive,
   susceptible

frajil   [frajeel] *adj* fragile

fraka   [fraka] *n* crash

frakti   [fraktee] *n* fracture

fran   [franh] *adj* frank, candid

frape   [frapeh] *v* hit, bang, knock; strike,
   hurt

frè {depans} *n* **fee(s)**

frè   [freh] *n* brother

fredi   [fredee] *n* cold

frekan   [frehkanh] rude, fresh

frennen   [frenhnenh] *v* stop

frèt   [freht] *adj* cold, cool

freyè, laperèz   fright

fri   [fhree] *v* fry

frijidè   [fhreejeedeh] *n* refrigerator

friksyonen   [freekseeonenh] *v* massage, rub

fripit   [freepit] *n* fly, bug

57

fristrasyon   [freestrasyonh] *n* frustration
fròd   [fraud] *n* fraud
fromaj   [fwomaj] *n* cheese
frontyè   [fwonteeheh] *n* border
frote   [fwotay] *v* rub, chafe, scrub
fuit   [fuit] *n* leak
fwa   [fwa] *n* liver; faith
fwi   [fwee] *n* fruit
fyè   [fyeh] *adj* proud
fyète   [fyehteh] *n* pride

G

gad [gahd] *n* guard, soldier
gade [gahdeh] *v* look, peek, glance
gadmanje [gahdmanhjeh] *n* pantry
gaga [gaga] *adj* imbecile, dumb
gagòt [gahgot] *n* fuss
gaj, *v* **garagti** pledge
galata [gahlahtah] *n* attic, loft
galèt [gahlet] *n* stone
galon [gahlonh] *n* gallon
galope [galogpay] *v* gallop, canter
gan [ganh] *n* glove
garaj [gahraj] *n* garage
garanti [gahranhtee] *v* warrant, guaranty
gason [gasonh] *n* boy, male, man, *adj* strong
gaspiyaj [gahspeeyahj] *n* waste
gaspiye [gahspeeyeh] *v* waste, squander
gate [gahteh] *adj* bad, spoiled, *v* spoil
gato [gahto] *n* cake
gayan [gahyanh] *n* winner
gaye [gahyeh] *v* spread
gaye [gahyeh] *v* dissipate, spread; arise
gaz [gas] *n* fuel

gazon [gahzonh] *n* lawn

gedj [gauge] *n/v* gauge

gen pitye [genh pityeh] *adj* merciful, clement

gen mwayen [genh mwayenh] *v* afford

gen konesans [genh konaysanhs] *adj* conscious

gen vètij [genh vehtij] *adj* dizzy

gen kouraj [gen kooraj] *adj* strong

gen lentansyon [genh lenhtanhsyonh] *v* intend

genlè [genhleh] *adv* apparently, *v* appear

genyen [genhyenh] *n* to have, earn, own; win

gèp [gep] *n* hornet, wasp

gid [geed] *n* guide

gide [geedeh] *v* guide

gildiv [geeldeev] *n* still

glas [glass] *n* ice, frost; mirror

glase [glaseh] *adj* cold;

glasi [glasee] *n* concrete pad

glise [gleeseh] *v* slide, creep, glide, slip

glòb [glob] *n* globe

glorifye [gloreefyeh] *v* glorify, praise

gòch [gosh] *adj* clumsy, left, awkward

gode [goday] *n* cup

gòj   [goj] *n* throat

gòje   [gojeh] gulp

gòlf   [golf] *n* golf, bay

gonfle   [gonhflay] *v* inflate; bulge, *n*
  indigestion

gonm   [gonhm] *n* glue; chewing gum

gonmen   [gonhmenh] *v* glue, *adj* sticky

gou   [goo] *n* flavor, savor, taste

goumen   [goomenh] *n* quarrel, *v* fight,
  struggle

goumen   [goomenh] *n* brawl, *v* fight

gout   [goot] *n* drop

goute   [gooteh] *v* taste; snack

gouvène   [goovehneh] *v* govern

gra   [grah] *adj* fat, plump

grad   [grad] *n* grade, rank, diploma

grafouyen   [grafooyenh] *v* scratch

graje   [grahjeh] *v* scrape, grate

gran   [granh] *adj* large, big; famous

gran   [granh] *adj* great, large

gran-papa   [granhpapa] *n* grandfather

grandi   [granhdee] *v* grow

grangou   [grungoo] *adj* avid; hungry; eager

grangou   [granhgoo] *n* famine

granmoun   [granhmoon] *n* adult, elder,
  mature

grann [gran] *n* grandmother

grap [grahp] *n* bunch, cluster

grate [grateh] *v* scrape

grate [grahteh] *v* scratch itch

gratèl [grahtel] *n* itch

gratis [grahtis] *adj* free

grav [grahv] *adj* grave

gravye [grahvyeh] *n* gravel

grenn pa grenn [grenpagren] *adv* individually

grenn [gren] *n* grain, unit, *adj* single

grenn [gren] *n* seed, berry; cachet, pill; testicle

grenpe [grenhpay] *v* climb

grès kochon [grehs koshonh] lard

grès [gress] *n* grease, fat

grese [grehseh] *v* grease

gri [gree] *adj* gray; tipsy

grif [grief] *n* paw

grif [grief] *n* claw

grip [greep] *n* flu, cold

griye [greeyeh] *v* roast; parch

griye [greeyeh] *v* roast

griyen [greeyenh] *v* giggle

gro [papa, manman} *adj* huge

gronde [gwonhdeh] *v* rumble, roar; frown

grosè [gwoseh] *n* size, dimension

grosoulye [gwosoolyeh] *adj* rude
grosye [gwosyeh] *adj* crude, gross
gròt [grot] *n* grotto, cave
gwòs [gross] *adj* expecting, pregnant; with
   child
gwoup [gwoop] *n* group
gwoupe [gwoopeh] *v* group

i

idantifye [eedantifyeh] *v* identify
idyo [eedeeo] *adj/n* idiot, blockhead, daft
ijyèn [eejyehn] *n* hygiene
il [eel] *n* island
ilejitim [eelehjeeteem] *adj* illegitimate
imaj [eemaj] *n* image
imajinasyon [eemajeenasyonh] *n*
  imagination
imajine [imahjeeneh] *v* imagine; picture,
  fancy
imanite [eemaneeteh] *n* humanity, human
  kind
imans [eemans] *adj* immense
imedyat [eemehdyat] *adj* immediate
imen [eemen] *adj* human; considerate
imid [eemeed] *adj* humid
imitasyon [eemeetasyonh] *n* imitation
imite [eemeeteh] *v* imitate
imoral [eemorahl] *adj* immoral
imòtèl [eemotel] *adj* immortal
inegal [inehgahl] *adj* unequal, uneven
ini [eenee] *v* unite, *adj* united

inifye [eeneefyeh] *v* unify
inisyal [eeneesyahl] *adj* initial, first
inite [eeneeteh] *n* unit; unity
inondasyon [eenondahsyonh] *n* innundation, deluge
inonde [eenondeh] *v* flood
inosan [eenosanh] *adj* innocent
inyon [eenyonh] *n* union, marriage
irige [eereegeh] *v* irrigate
irite [eerietay] *v* irritate, chafe
isit [eeseet] *adv* here
istansil [istanhseel] *n* utensil
istwa [istwa] *n* story, fable, tale
itil [eeteel] *adj* handy, useful
itilite [eetiliteh] *n* utility, usefulness
itilize [eetilizeh] *v* use
izaje [eezajeh] *adj* used
ize [eezeh] *adj* used
izin [eezeen] *n* factory, manufacture

J

jaden   [jahdenh] *n* produce garden, plot, cultivated land

jaden flè   [jahdenh fleh] *n* decorative garden

jadinye   [jahdeenyeh] *n* gardener

jagon   [jahgonh] *n* jargon, slang

jako   [jahko] *n* parrot

jalou   [jahloo] *adj* jealous

jamè   [jahmeh] *adv* never

janbon   [janhbonh] *n* ham

jandam   [jhanhdam] *n* cop, guard

janm   [janhm] *n* leg, *adv* never

janti   [janhtee] *adj* gentle, kind, polite

janvye   [janhvyeh] *n* January

jape   [japeh] *v* bark

je   [jeh] *n* eye; articulation, joint

jedi   [jehdee] *n* Thursday

jefò   [jhefoh] *n* effort

jele   [jehleh] *n* jelly

jemi   [jehmee] *v* moan, wail, whimper

jen   [jenh] *n* June

jèn   [jehn] *adj* young

jeneral   [jehnehrahl] *adj/n* general

jenere [jehnehreh] *adj* generous, *v* generate
jenès [jehness] *n* youth; prostitute
jenèz [jehnez] *n* genesis
jenn [jhen] *adj* young
jennjan [jhenjanh] *n* lad
jenou [jehnoo] *n* knee
jepete [jepateh] *adj* blind
jeyan [jehyanh] *adj* giant
ji [jhee] *n* juice
jij [jheej] *n* judge
jije [jheejeh] *v* judge
jijman [jeehjmanh] *n* verdict
jimo [jheemo] *n/adj* twin
jip [jheep] *n* skirt
jiri [jheeree] *n* jury
jis [jhees] *adj* just, appropriate, fair
jiska (jis, jouk) [jheeska] *prp* till
jiskaske [jheeskaskeh] *prp* until
jistifye [jeestifieh] *v* justify
jistis [jeestis] *n* justice
jiyè [jheeyeh] *n* July
jodi [jhodee] today
jòn [jonn] *adj* yellow
jònze [jonnzeh] *n* yolk
jou [jhoo] *n* day, daylight
joumou [jhoomoo] *n* squash

jounal [jhoonal] *n* newspaper, diary/log
jounen [jhoonenh] *n* daytime
joure [jooreh] *v* blame, admonish; insult
jovyal [jhovyal] *adj* mellow
jwe ak [jweh ak] *v* fiddle
jwe [jweh] *v* play
jwenn [jwen] *v* find
jwèt [jwet] *n* game, toy
jwi [jwee] *v* enjoy
jwif [jweef] *adj* jewish

K

ka   [kah] *n* case; quart, quarter
kab   [kab] *n* telegram; cable, wire
kabann   [kaban] *n* bed
kabicha   [kahbeesha] *v* nap
kabin   [kabeen] *n* cabin
kabinè   [kabeeneh] *n* office; toilet, *v* bowel
  movement
kabrit   [kahbrit] *n* goat
kabwèt   [kabwet] *n* carriage
kach   [cash] *n* cash
kache   [cachet] *v* conceal, hide
kadans   [kadanhs] *n* cadence
kadav   [kadav] *n* cadaver, corpse
kadna   [kahdna] *n* lock, padlock
kadnase   [kahdnahseh] *v* lock
kado   [kahdo] *n* gift, present
kafe   [cafe] *n* coffee; bar, pub
kajole   [kajholay] *v* cajole, coax
kakas   [kakas] *n* carcass
kalamite   [kalameetay] *n* calamity
kalbas   [kahlbas] *n* squash
kale   [kaley] *v* beat, peel

kalite [kalitay] *n* attribute, quality, *adj* such
kalkile [kalkeelay] *v* calculate, think
kalm [kalm] *adj* calm
kalmason [kahlmahsonh] *n* snail
kalòj [kalohj] *n* cage
kalomnye [kahlomnyeh] *v* defame, slander
kalonnen [kahlonenh] *v* pelt, pound
kalòt [kahlot] *n* slap
kamera [kameyra] *n* camera
kanape [canape] *n* couch
kanbriyole [kanhbreeyoleh] *v* burglarize
kanistè [canister] *n* canister
kanmarad [kanhmarad] *n* comrade
kanmenm [kanhmenhm] *adv* indeed
kann [kahn] *n* sugar cane
kanna [kahna] *n* duck, *adj* crooked
kannay [kanhahy] *n* scoundrel
kanno [kanhno] *n* gun
kanpe [kanhpeh] *v* stand, raise
kanpman [kampmanh] *n* camp
kansè [kanhseh] *n* cancer
kanson [kanhsonh] slacks
kantin [kanhteen] *n* canteen
kantite [kanhteeteh] *n* quantity
kaoutchou [kawotshoe] *n* tire, rubber
kap [cap] *n* kite

kapab   [khapab] *adj* able, capable, *v* can
kapasite   [kapasitay] *n* capacity
kapital   [kapital] *adj/n* capital
kapon   [kaponh] *adj/n* coward
kapris   [kahprees] *n* fad, whim
kaptif   [kaptif] *adj* captive
kaptire   [kapteeray] *v* capture
kaptive   [kaptiveh] *v* captivate
karakteristik   [characteristic] *n* characteristic
karakterize   [characterizeh] *v* characterize
karant   [kahranht] *adj* forty
kare   [karay] *adj* square; bold; audacious
karès   [kahress] *n* caress
karòt   [kahrot] *n* carrot
karyè   [karyeh] *n* career; quarry
kase   [kahsey] *v* break
kasròl   [kahswol] *n* pan
kat   [kat] *adj* four, *n* card; map
katedral   [katehdral] *n* cathedral
katreven   [kahtrehvenh] *adj* eighty
katrevendis   [kahtrevenhdis] *adj* ninety
katye   [kahtyeh] *n* quarter, neighborhood
kav   [kav] *n* cellar
kavya   [kavya] *n* caviar, ze pwason
kaw   [kaw] *n* crow, raven

kay [caille] *n* house, dwelling

kaye [kayeh] *n* notebook, *v* curdle, *adj* complex

kazwèl [kahzwell] *adj* timid, bashful

ke bèf [kehbef] *n* oxtail

kè [keh] *n* heart, centre

kèk [kehk] *adj* some, a few

kèlkeswa [kelkeswa] *prn* whatever

kenbe [kenhbeh] *v* (with)hold, arrest, detain, keep; ontend

kenz [kenhz] *adj* fifteen

kèplen [kehplenh] nausea, qualm

kès [kess] *n* box, case

kesyon [kehsyonh] *n* question

kesyone [kehsyoneh] *v* question

keyi [kehyee] *v* harvest, pick

kibò [keeboh] *adv* where

kidnape [kidnapeh] *v* abduct

kidonk [keedonk] *adv* whence

kijan [keejhanh] *adv* how

kikote [keekoteh] *adv* where

kilè [keeleh] *adv* when

kilès [keeless] *adj* which, who

kilt [kilt] *n* cult

kilti [kiltee] *n* culture

kim [keem] *n* suds

kimoun   [keemoon] *prn* who
kin   [kin] paran
kirye   [kiryeh] *adj* curious
kisa   [keesah] *adj* what
kite   [keeteh] *v* abandon, leave
kiyè   [keeyeh] *n* spoon
kizin   [keezeen] *n* kitchen
kizinyè   [keezeenyeh] *n* cook
klakxonn   [klaxon] *n* horn
klarifye   [klarifyeh] *v* clarify
klas   [class] *n* class
lase   [klahseh] *v* classify; file
kle   [kleh] *n* key
klè   [kleh] *adj* clear, explicit
klè   [kleh] *adj* clear, distinct, transparent
klèje   [klehjeh] *n* clergyman
klere   [klereh] *adj* bright, shiny, *v* flash, shine, sparkle
klik   [click] *n* gang
klima   [kleemah] *n* weather
klòch   [klosh] *n* bell
kloròks   [clorox] *n* bleach
klou   [kloo] *n* nail
kloure   [klooreh] *v* nail
kò   [koh] *n* body
koabite   [koabeeteh] *v* cohabit

kòb   [kob] *n* money
kòche   [kosheh] *v* abrade, scrape
kochon   [kohshonh] *n* pig, swine
kòd   postal zip
kòd   [kod] *n* cord, rope, string
kodak   [kokak] *n* camera
kodenn   [kohden] *n* turkey
koefisyan   [koefiseeanh] *n* coefficient
kòf   [koff] *n* trunk
kòfrefò   [kofrehfoh] *n* safe
kòk   [cock] *n* rooster; penis
koken   [kohkenh] *n* rascal, knave
koki   [kohkee] *n* shell
koklich   [koklish] *n* red eye
kòkraze   [kohkrazeh] *n* lassitude, *adj* sore
kòl   [kol] *n* collar
kola   [kola] *n* kola
kolabore   [kolaboreh] *v* collaborate
kolasyon   [kolaseeonh] *n* breakfast
kole   [kohleh] *v* stick,
kòlè   [koleh] *n* anger, bile
kolèj   [kohlehj] *n* college
kolekte   [kolekteh] *v* collect
koli   [kohlee] *n* package
kolòn   [kohlon] *n* column
kolonèl   [kohlonel] colonel *n*

74

kolore [kohloreh] *v* color, dye
kolore [kohlohreh] *v* color
kòman [kohmanh] *adv* how
kòmande [komanhdeh] *v* command, order
kòmande [komanhdeh] *v* order
kòmann [koman] *n* order
kòmann [koman] *n* command
kòmanse [komanhseh] *v* begin, commence; start
komen [kohmenh] *adj* common
komès [kohmess] *n* commerce, business
komèt [kohmet] *n* comet, *v* commit
komi [kohmee] *n* clerk
komik [komeek] *adj* silly
komik [kohmik] *adj* funny, *n* cartoon
kominike [kominikeh] *v* communicate, *n* communiqué
komisyon [kohmeesyonh] *n* errand; commission
kòn [konn] *n* horn
kondane [konhdaneh] *v* condemn
kondiktè [kodikteh] *n* driver
kondisyon [konhdeeseeonh] *n* condition
kondui [konhdui] *v* drive
konduit [konhduit] *n* conduct
konekte [kohnekteh] *v* connect

75

konesans   [kohnesanhs] *n* knowledge;
  acquaintance
kònèy   [konehy] *n* crow
konfese   [konhfeseh] *v* confess
konfime   [konhfimeh] *v* confirm
konfiti   [konhfeetee] *n* preserve
konfizyon   [konhfizyonh] *n* confusion
konfò   [konfoh] *n* comfort, amenity
konfòme   [konhfomeh] *v* conform
konfòtab   [konhfotab] *adj* comfortable
konje   [konhjeh] *n* holiday
konjeste   [conhjesteh] *adj* congested, *v*
  congest
konjle   [konhjleh] *v* freeze, *adj* frozen
konjwen   [konhjwenh] *n* spouse, companion
konkeri   [konhkeree] *v* conquer
konkli   [konhklee] *v* conclude
konkonm   [konhkom] *n* cucumber
konkou   [konhkoo] *n* competition, contest;
  assistance
konnen   [konhnenh] *v* know
konpare   [konhpareh] *v* compare
konpayon   [konhpayonh] *n* companion,
  escort
konpetan   [konhpetanh] *adj* capable,
  competent

konpetisyon [konhpeteeseeonh] *n*
competition, contest

konplè [konhpleh] *n* outfit, suit

konplèt [konhplet] *adj* complete

konplete [konhpleteh] *v* complete

konplètman [konhpletmanh] *adv*
completely, wholly

konplike [konhpleekeh] *adj* complicated, *v*
complicate

konplote [konhploteh] *v* plot

konpòte [konhpoteh] *v* behave

konpoze [konhpozeh] *n* mixture, compound

konpoze [konhpozeh] *v* compose; take an
examination

konprann [konhpran] *n* wit, understanding,
v understand

konprann [konhpran] *v* comprehend,
understand

konsanti [konhsanhtee] *v* agree, consent

konsekans [konhsehkanhs] *n* consequence

konsèp [konhsep] *n* concept

konsèy [konhsehy] *n* advice, council

konsèye [konhsehyeh] *n* counselor

konsidere [konhsidereh] *v* consider

konsilte [konhsilteh] *v* to be examined,
consult

konsiste   [konhsisteh] *v* consist
konsole   [konhsohle] *v* console
konsolide   [konhsolideh] *v* consolidate
konsonmen   [konhsonhmenh] *n* soup, *v* consume
konstan   [konhtanh] *adj* constant
konstant   [konhstant] *n* constant
konstitye   [konhstityeh] *v* constitute
konstrui   [konhstwi] *v* construct
konstwi   [konstwee] *v* build
konsyans   [konhsyanhs] *n* conscience
kont   [konht] *adj* enough, plenty
kont   [kont] *prp* against
kont   [kont] *n* account, tale
kont   [konht] *n* tale
kontamine   [konhtamineh] *v* contaminate
kontan   [konhtanh] *n* cash
kontan   [konhtanh] *adj* happy, jolly, glad
kontanple   [konhtanpleh] *v* contemplate, gaze, behold
kontante   [konhtanteh] *v* satisfy
kontantman   [konhtantmanh] *n* delight, joy
konte   [konhteh] *v* count
konte   [konteh] *v* count
kontinye   [kontinyeh] *v* continue
kontinye   [konhteenyeh] *v* continue, proceed

kontni   [kontnee] *n* content
kontòsyone   [konhtoseeoneh] *v* contort
kontoune   [kontooneh] *v* bypass
kontra   [konhtra] *n* contract
kontraryete   [konhtraryehteh] *n* chagrin,
   aggravation; orry
kontrè   [kontreh] *adj* opposed contrary
kontredi   [konhtredee] *v* contradict,
   contravene
kontrekare   [konhtrekareh] *v* challenge
kontrenn   [konhtren] *v* constrain, coerce
kontrenn   [konhstren] *v* constrain
kontribye   [konhtribyeh] *v* contribute
konvalesans   [konhvalehsanhs] *n* remission
konvansyon   [kohnvahnsionh] *n* convention
konvenk   [kohnvenk] *v* convince
konvèsasyon   [kohnvehsasionh] *n*
   conversation
konvnab   [konhvnab] *adj* convenient, proper
konvoke   [konhvokeh] *v* summon, convene
konvwate   [konhvwahteh] lust
konyak   [cognac] *n* cognac
konyensidans   [konhhensidanhs] *n*
   coincidence
kopi   [kohpee] *n* copy
kopye   [kohpyeh] *v* copy, imitate

kòrèk [korrek] *adj* correct

koresponn [kohrespon] *v* face up,
  correspond; challenge

koridò [kohreedoh] *n* hall

korije [kohreejeh] *v* correct, amend

kòronp [korronmp] *v* bribe; corrupt

koryas [kohrias] *adj* coarse, rugged, tough

kostim [kohsteem] *n* suit

kòt [kot] *n* rib

kote [kohteh] *n* side

kote [kohteh] *adv* where, *adj* next to

kote , *v* place

koton [kohtonh] *v* cotton

kou [koo] *n* neck; blow, hit, *adv* like

koube [koobeh] *v* bend, *adj* bent

kouche [koosheh] *v* lay down

koud [kood] *v* sew, *n* elbow

koukou [cuckoo] *n* owl

koule [kooley] *v* flow; dive; sink

koulè [kooleh] *n* color

koulèv [koolev] *n* snake, serpent

kounye-a [koonyeh-a] *adv* now, presently

koup [koop] *n* couple; cut (hair, clothing)

koupab [koopab] *adj* guilty, *n* convict

koupe [koopeh] *v* cut, chop, incise

kouraj [kooraj] *n* courage, strength, mettle

kouran [kooranh] *adj* current; fluent, *n* current

kourandè [kooranhdeh] *n* draft

kouri dèyè [kooree dehyeh] *v* chase

kouri [kooree] *v* run

kous [koos] *n* race

kousen [koosenh] *n* cushion

kout [koot] *adj* short; concise

koutcha [kootcha] *n* style, manner; culture

koute [kooteh] *v* cost

koutfwèt [koofwet] *n* lash

koutim [kootim] *n* custom

koutiryè [kooteeryeh] *n* dressmaker

koutje [kootjeh] *n* look

kouto [kooto] *n* knife

koutpwen [kootpwenh] *n* jab

koutwa [kootwa] *adj* courteous

koutye [kootyeh] *n* broker

kouvèti [koovettee] *n* cover, lid; blanket, quilt

kouvri [koovree][*v* cover, coat; hide

kòz [koz] *n* cause

koze [kohzeh] *n* conversation, chat, rumor, *v* alk, converse

krache [krasheh] *n/v* spit, saliva

krak [krak] *n* crack

81

krake   [krakeh] *v* creak, split
kranpon   [kranhponh] *n* clamp
krapo   [krapo] *n* frog
kras   [crass] *n* dirt, scum
kravat   [kravat] *n* tie
kraze   [krazey] *v* break, *adj* broken, destroyed, rashed
kraze   [krahzeh] *v* mash, squash, snash
kre   [kreh] *adj* hollow
kredi   [krehdee] *n* credit
kredite   [krehdeeteh] *v* credit
krèm   [krehm] *n* cream
kretyen   [kretyenh] *adj* christian; being
kreyati   [krehati] *n* creature,
kreye   [krehyeh] *v* create
kreyon   [krehyonh] *n* pencil
kri   [kree] *adj* raw, crude
kribich   [kreebish] *n* shrimp, crayfish
krich   [kreesh] *n* jug, pitcher
krim   [kreem] *n* crime
kriminel   [criminel] *n* felon, *adj* criminal
kripya   [kreepya] *adj* avaricious, selfish
kripya   [kreepya] *adj* stingy
krisifye   [kreesifyeh] *v* crucify
kriye   [kriyeh] *v* cry, sob, weep
kriyèl   [kreeyehl] *adj* cruel

krochi   [kwoshee] *adj* askew, bent
krout   [kroot] *n* crumb, crust
krout   [kroot] *n* scab
kui   [kui] *n* leather
kuis   [kuis] *n* thigh
kuiv   [kuiv] copper
kwa   [kwa] *n* cross
kwafè   [kwafeh] *n* barber
kwaze   [kwazeh] *v* cross, breed
kwazyè   [kwazyeh] *n* cruise
kwè   [kweh] *v* believe, trust
kwen   [kwenh] *n* corner
kwense   [kwenseh] *v* corner
kwòk   [kwok] *n* fang, hook
kwoke   [kwokeh] *v* hug, embrace; hook

L

la   [lah] *adv* here
la kochon   [lahkoshon] *n* bacon
labank   [lahbanhk] *n* bank
labou   [laboo] *n* mud
labrim   [labrim] *n* mist
labrin   [labreen] *n* dusk
lachas   [lahshass] *n* hunting
lacho   [lasho] *n* lime
ladesant   [ladessant] *n* shelter, lodging
ladwan   [ladwan] *n* custom
lafimen   [lafeemenh] *n* smoke
lafwa   [lafwa] *n* faith
lafyèv   [lafyehv] *n* fever
lage   [lahgay] *v* drop; let go, quit; forsake
lagè   [lageh] *n* war
lagras   [lagrass] *n* grace
laj   [lahj] *n* age
laj   [lahj] *adj* large, broad, wide
lajan   [lahjanh] *n* currency, money
lajenès   [lahjehness] *n* youth
lajistis   [lajeestis] *n* justice
lak   [lak] *n* lake

lakay   [lahkahy] *n* home
lakizin   [lahkeezeen] *n* kitchen
lakòl   [lakol] *n* glue
lakou   [lakoo] *n* yard, court
lakòz   [lakoz] *n* cause, reason
lakre   [lakreh] chalk *n*
lalin   [laleen] *n* moon
lalwa   [lalwa] *n* law
lam   [lam] *n* blade, wave
lamòd   [lamod] *n* fashion, vogue
lanbe   [lanhbeh] *v* lick
lanbinen   [lanhbeenenh] *v* dally, dawdle
lane   [lahneh] *n* year, *adv* yearly
lanèj   [lanehj] *n* snow
lanfè   [lanhfeh] *n* hell
lang   [lang] *n* language, tongue
lank   [lanhk] *n* ink
lanmè   [lanhmeh] *n* sea
lannuit   [lanhnuit] *n* night
lantèman   [lanhtehmanh] *n* funeral, burial
lantouray   [lanhtoorahy] *n* fence; surrounding
lapè   [lapeh] *n* peace
lapèch   [lapesh] *n* fishing, catch
lapen   [lahpenh] *n* rabbit
lapenn   [lahpen] *n* grief, sorrow
laplenn   [lahplen] *n* plain, countryside

lapli [laplee] *n* rain
lapòs [lahpos] *n* post office
laprès press
lari [laree] n street
larouze [laroozeh] *n* dew
lasajès [lasahjess] *n* wisdom
lasante [lahsanhteh] *n* health
lasisiy [laseesiy] *n* enticement, seduction, lure, *v* tantalize
lasosyete [lahsosyeteh] *n* society
lasoup [lahsoup] *n* soup
latè [lahteh] *n* Earth
laterè [lahtehreh] *n* terror
lavant [lavant] *n* sale
lave [lahveh] *v* wash
laverite [lahveriteh] *n* truth
lavi [lavee] *n* life
lavil [lahveal] *n* town, downtown
lay [lahy] *n* garlic
lè [leh] *n* air;
lè [leh] *n* hour, time; *adv* when
lèd [lead] *adj* ugly
legim [legim] *n* vegetable, produce
legliz [lehgliz] *n* church
lejand [lejanhd] *n* caption; legend, *adj* untrue

leje   [lehjeh] *adj* light
lekòl   [lehkol] *n* school
lekti   [lektee] *n* reading
lemonn   [lehmon] *n* world
lendi   [lenhdee] *n* Monday
lenmi   [lenmee] *n* enemy, foe
lenn   [len] *n* blanket, linen; wool
lentansyon   [lenhtanhsyonh] *n* intent
lepase   [lehpaseh] *n* past
lès   [less] *n* east
lese   [lehseh] *v* leave, quit
lesiv   [lehsiv] *n* laundry, wash
leson   [lessonh] *n* lesson
lesovè   [lehsohveh] *n* savior
lespri   [lespree] *n* mind, spirit
lespwa   [lesspwa] *n* hope
lèt   [let] *n* milk; letter
leta   [lehta] *n* state, government
lete   [lehteh] *n* summer
lètkaye   [lehtkayeh] *n* milk curd
leton   [lehtonh] *n* brass
lèv   [lev] *n* lip
levanjil   [levanhjeel] *n* gospel
leve   [lehveh] *v* lift, raise; protrude
leve kanpe   [levehkanhpeh] *v* rise
leven   [lehvenh] *n* yeast

leza   [lezah] *n* lizard

li   [lee] *v* read

li   [lee] *prn* he; she; it; him; her; -its, his, her

li-menm   [leemenhm] *prn* (him/her/it/) self

lib   [leeb] *adj* free

libere   [leebehreh] *v* free, release

libète   [leebehte] *n* freedom

likid   [likid] *n* fluid, liquid

limanite   [leemaneeteh] *n* mankind, humanity

limen   [leemenh] *v* turn on, *adj* on

limit   [limit] *n* limit

limyè   [leemyeh] *n* light

lis   [lis] *n* list, *adj* smooth

lisans, pèmi, *v* **pèmèt**   permit

lisid   [lisid] *adj* lucid, sane

lit   [lit] *n* struggle

lite   [leeteh] *v* struggle, wrestle

liv   [leave] *n* book; pound

livè   [leeveh] *n* winter

liy   [leey] *n* line, lane

lizib   [lizib] *adj* legible

lizyè   [leezeeheh] *n* border, limit

lò   [loh] *n* gold

lòd   [lod] *n* order, command

lòdè   [lohdeh] *n* odor
loje   [lojeh] *v* accommodate
lokal   [lokahl] *adj* local, domestic
lokalize   [lokaleezeh] *v* locate
lokatè   [lokateh] *n* tenant
lonbraj   [lonhbrahj] *n* shade, shadow
lonè   [loneh] *n* honor
long   [long] *adj* long
longè   [lonhgeh] *n* length
lopital   [lohpitahl] *n* hospital
loray   [lorahy] *n* thunder
loseyan   [losehyanh] *n* ocean
lòt   [lot] *adj* other
lòtbò   [lotboh] *adv* abroad, beyond
lote   [lohteh] *v* allot
lotè   [loteh] *n* author, agent, cause
lotòn   [lotohn] *n* autumn, fall
lotri   [lotree] *n* lottery
lou   [loo] *adj* heavy
louch   [loosh] *n* ladle
louvri   [loovree] *v* open
luil   [luil] *n* oil
luile   [luileh] *v* oil
lwa   [lwa] *n* law, rule; god, saint
lwaye   [lwayeh] *n* lease, rental
lwazi   [lwazee] *n* leisure

lwe [lweh] *v* rent
lwen [lwenh] *adj* far, remote; austere, *adv*
  away
lwès [lwess] *n* west
lyas [lhyass] *n* bundle
lyen [lyenh] *n* link
lyezon [liayzonh] *n* affair, link
lyon [lyonh] *n* lion

M

ma   [mah] *n* coffee grounds
mach   [mash] *n* stair step
machandaj   [mashanhdahj] *n* bargaining
machande   [mashanhdeh] *v* bargain, haggle
mache   [masheh] *n* market, *v* walk; chew
machin   [machine] *n* vehicle, machine
machwa   [machwa] *n* jaw
madanm   [madam] *n* lady, woman, wife
madi   [mahdee] *n* Tuesday
madjigridji   [magigreegi] *v* scribble
magazen   [magazenh] *n* store, shop
magouy   [mahgooy] *n* enigma, mystery
magouyè   [mahgooyeh]*n* con, swindler
majik   [majeek] *adj* magic
majò   [mahjoh] *n* major
majore   [mahjoreh] *v* overcharge
mak   [mak] *n* mark, feature spot; make
makak   [makak] *n* monkey
make   [mahkeh] *v* mark, scratch
mal   [mahl] *adj* bad, wrong, *n* ache; male
malad   [malad] *adj* ill, sick
maladi   [maladee] *n* disease

maladwa   [maladwa] *adj* clumsy

malè   [mahleh] *n* misfortune

malediksyon   [malediikseeonh] *n* curse

malen   [mahlenh] *adj* cunning

malere   [mahlehreh] *n* indigent

malerezman   [mahlehrezmanh] *adv*
  unfortunately

malfini   [malfini] *n* hawk

malgre   [malgreh] *adv* although, despite

malis   [malis] *n* malice

malmennen   [malmenhnenh] *v* torture

malpwòp   [malpwop] *adj* nasty, dirty

maltèt   [maltet] *n* headache

maltrete   [maltrehteh] *v* mistreat, hurt, harm

mamè   [mahmeh] *n* nun

manch   [mansh] *n* sleeve

manda   [manhdah] *n* warrant; check;
  guarantee

mande   [manhdeh] *v* ask, demand; beg

mandyan   [manhdianh] *n* beggar

mani   [mahnee] *n* habit, vice

manifoul   [mahneefool] *n* manifold

maniskri   [maniskree] *n* manuscript

manje   [manhjeh] *v* eat, *n* aliment, food,
  meal, utrition

manje midi   [manhjeh meedee] *n* lunch

mank [manhk] *n* lack, shortage
manke [manhkeh] *v* lack, miss
manm [manhm] *n* member
manman [mahnmahn] *n* mother, *adj* enormous, huge
mannken [mankenh] *n* mannequin
mansyon [manhsyonh] *n* mansion; mention
mansyone [manhsyoneh] *v* mention
mant [manht] *n* mint
mantal [manhtal] *adj* mental
mantè [manhteh] *n* liar
manti [mahtee] *n* lie, *adj* false
manton [manhtonh] *n* chin
manyak [mahniahk] *adj/n* maniac
manyèl [mahnyehl] *n* book, manual, *adj* manual
manyen [manhyenh] *v* touch, handle; manipulate
mare [mahreh] *v* tie, unite; fasten
marekaj [mahrehkahj] *n* marsh, swamp
mari [mahree] *n* husband
maron [mahwonh] *adj* brown; escaped, *v* escape
maryaj [mahriaj] *n* marriage
marye [mahryeh] *v* marry, couple
mas [mass] *n* mass, lump

mas [mass] *n* March
mask [mask] *n* mask, cloak
mat [mat] *adj* dull
matant [mahtanht] *n* aunt
match [match] *n* match
aten [mahtenh] *n* morning
matènite [mahtehniteh] *n* maternity
materyèl [mahteryel] *n/adj* material
materyo [mahteryo] *n* material
matla [mahtla] *n* mattress
matlo [mahtlo] *n* seaman
mato [mahto] *n* hammer
matyè [mahtyeh] *n* matter; fecal matter
mayi [mayee] *n* corn, maize
me [meh] *n* May
mèb [meb] *n* furniture
mechan [mehsahnh] *adj* cruel, mean,
   wicked
mefyans [mehfyanhs] *n* mistrust
mefye [mehfyeh] *v* beware, mistrust
mèki [mehkee] *n* mercury
mekontantman [mehkonhtanhtmanh] *n*
   discontent
mèkredi [mehkrehdee] *n* Wednesday
melanj [mehlanj] *n* mix
melanje [mehlanjeh] *v* mix; tangle

melimelo   [mehleemehlo] *n* fuss, disturbance
men   [menh] *conj* but; *adv* here!
men   [menh] *n* hand
menas   [mehnass] *n* menace, threat
menase   [mehnahseh] *v* threat
menm   [menhm] *adj* same
mennen   [menhnenh] *v* bring
menòt   [mehnot] *n* handcuffs
mens   [menhs] *adj* slim
mentni   [mentnee] *v* argue, maintain
mepri   [mehpri] *n* contempt
meprize   [mehprizeh] *v* despise, scorn
merit   [mehrit] *n* merit
merite   [meriteh] *v* deserve
mesaj   [mehsaj] *n* message
mesaje   [mehsajeh] *n* messenger
mesye   [mehsyeh] *n* mister, man
mete   [mehteh] *v* put, wear
mèt   [met] *n* teacher; owner; meter; meter
   stick
mèt   [met] *v* may
mètkay   [mehtkahy] *n* host, owner
metrès   [mehtress] *n* mistress
mètri   [mehtree] *v* bruise
metye   [mehtyeh] *n* trade
mèvèy   [mehvey] *n* wonder

meyè   [mehyeh] *adj* better
mezi   [mehzee] *n* measure
mezire   [mehzeereh] *v* measure
mi   [mee] *n* wall, *adj* mature, ripe
midi   [midi] *n* noon
mil   [mil] *adj* thousand
min   [mean] *n* mine
minè   [meaneh] *n/adj* minor
minrè   [meanreh] *n* ore
mirak   [mirak] *n* miracle
mis   [miss] *n* nurse, Ms.
misk   [misk] *n* musk, brawn
miskle   [miskleh] *adj* muscular, brawny, hefty
mistik   [meestik] *adj* mysterious
misyon   [meesyonh] *n* assignment, mission
mitan   [meetanh] *n* center, heart; middle
miwa   [miwa] *n* mirror
miwate   [miwateh] *v* gleam
miyò   [meeyoh] *adj/adv* better
mizè   [meezeh] *n* misery, wretch
mizerab   [meezerab] *adj* miserable, wretched
mo   [mo] *n* word
mò   [moh] *n* cadaver, dead
mòde   [mohdeh] *v* bite
modèl   [mohdel] *n* model, pattern

modele [modleh] *v* model, pattern
modere [mohdereh] *adj* moderate
modès [mohdess] *adj* modest, humble
modi [modee] *v* curse, damn, *adj* cursed
mòflè [muffleh] *n* exhaust
moke [mohkeh] *v* mock
mòksis [moksis] *adj* gloomy, sullen
moleste [mohlesteh] *v* molest
moman [mohmanh] *n* moment, instant
mòn [monn] *n* hill, mount, mountain
monnen [monhenh] *n* change
monnonk [monhnonhk] *n* uncle
mons [monhs] *n* monster
monsenyè [monhseyeh] *n* archbishop
mont [mont] *n* watch
montan [monhtanh] *n* amount, proceeds, total
monte (machin, chwal) ride
monte [monhteh] *v* ascend, climb *n* ascent
monte [monhteh] *v* lift, raise
montre [monhtreh] *v* show, indicate, teach, instruct
moso [mohso] *n* chunk, piece, part
motè [mohteh] *n* motor
mou [moo] *adj* soft
mouch [moosh] *n* fly

mouche   [moosheh] *v* wipe/blow nose, *n*
  man; husband

mouchwa   [mooshwa] *n* handkerchief

moulen   [moolenh] *v* grind; chew, *n* grinder;
  mill

moumou   [moomoo] *n* bathrobe

moun   [moon] *n* person, individual

mouri   [mooree] *adj* dead, *v* die, deaden,
  diminish

moustach   [moustache] *n* moustache

moustik   [moostik] *n* mosquito

mouton   [mootonh] *n* sheep, lamb, mutton

mouvman   [moovmanh] *n* movement,
  motion

mouye   [mooyeh] *adj* wet, moist

move   [mohveh] *adj* bad, mean, unhappy;
  evil

movezè   [mohvehzeh] *n* (bad) spirit

mwa   [mwa] *n* month

mwat   [mwat] *adj* moist, damp

mwatye   [mwatyeh] *n* half

mwayen   [mwayenh] *n* means, *adj* average

mwayèn   [mwayehn] *n* average, mean;
  capacity

mwen   [mwenh] *prn* I, me, my

mwenn   [mwen] *adj* least

mwens   [mwenhs] *adj* less
mye   [myeh] *adv* better
myèl   [myehl] *n* bee
myèt   [myeht] *n* crumb

N

naje   [nahjeh] *v* swim
nan   [nanh] *prp* in, into
nandòmi   [nanhdohmee] *adj* asleep
nanm   [nanhm] *n* soul
narin   [nahreen] *n* nostril
nasyon   [nahsyonh] *n* nation
natif-natal   [nateef-natal] *adj* local, native
navige   [nahveegeh] *v* sail
ne   [neh] *n* knot, node
nèf   [nef] *adj* nine; new
nèg   [neg] *n* fellow, man
neglijan   [nehgleejanh] *adj* negligent, lax
neglije   [nehgleejeh] *v* neglect
negòs   [negos] *n* commerce, business
nekoulan   [nehkoolanh] *n* noose
nemoni   [nehmonee] *n* pneumonia
nen   [nenh] *n* nose
nenpòt   [nenhpot] *adj* any; either
nenpòt kijan   [nenhpot keejanh] *adv*
   somehow
nesesè   [nehsehseh] *adj* necessary
nesesite   [necessiteh] *n* necessity

netwaye [nehtwayeh] *v* clean
neve [nehveh] *n* nephew
ni... ni [nee...nee] *conj* neither
nich [nish] *n* nest
nivle [neevleh] *v* grade, level
nivo [nivo] *n* level
nizans [nizanhs] *n* nuisance
non [nonh] *n* name, no {negation}
nonm [nonhm] *n* number; male companion
nonmen [nonhmenh] *v* name, nominate;
  appoint
nonsans [nonhsanhs] *n* nonsense
nosif [nosif] *adj* noxious
nosyon [nohsyonh] *n* notion
nòt [not] *n* note; entry
note [nohteh] *v* record, note, log
nou [noo] *prn* we, us, our
nouri [nooree] *v* feed, nourish
nouvèl [noovel] *n* news
nouvo [noovo] *adj* new, recent
novanm [nohvanhm] *n* November
noze [nohzeh] *n* nausea, qualm
nuaj [nuahj] *n* cloud
nuit [nuit] *n* night
nuizib [nuizib] *adj* annoying, bothersome
nwa [nwa] *adj* black, dark; *n* nut

nwaye   [nwayeh] *v* drown
Nwèl   [nwel] *n* Christmas

O

obeyi [obehyee] *v* obey
obeyisan [obehyeesanh] *adj* obedient
obèz [obez] *adj* obese
objè [objeh] *n* goal, purpose
objektif [objehkteef] *n* goal
oblije [obleejeh] *v* oblige, force
obsede [obsehdeh] *v* obsess, *adj* obsessed
obsèn [obsehn] *adj* obscene
obsève [obsehveh] *v* observe; reprimand
obstak [obstak] *n* obstacle
obstine [obstineh] *adj* obstinate
odasye [audasyeh] *adj* audacious
odè [audeh] *n* smell, scent; bouquet
odè [ohdeh] *n* odor, smell
òdinè [oddeeneh] *adj* ordinary, banal
òdone [ohdoneh] *v* order
òf [off] *n* offer, bid
ofans [ohfanhs] *n* offense
ofanse [ohfanhseh] *v* offend
òfelen [offehlenh] *n* orphan
ofisye [ohfeesyeh] *n* officer
ofri [ohfree] *v* offer

103

òganize [ohgahnizeh] *v* organize, arrange
ogmantasyon [ogmanhtahsyonh] *n* increase
ogmante [ohgmanhteh] *v* augment, add,
  increase
okazyon [ohkahzyonh] *n* occasion,
  opportunity
okenn kote [ohken kohteh] *adv* nowhere
okenn [oken] *adj* no, none
okèt [ohket] *n* hiccup
okipe [okeepeh] *v* handle; occupy, *adj* busy
okouran [ohkouranh] *adv* abreast
oktòb [ohktob] *n* October
òl [all] *n* hall
oliv [ohliv] olive
olye [ohlyeh] *prp* instead
omilye [ohmeelye] *n* center, middle
òne [ohneh] *v* adorn, decorate
onèt [ohnet] *adj* honest, proper
onfwa [onhfwa] *adv* once
onka [onhkah] *adj* quarter, quart
onlòt [onhlot] *adj/prn* another
onz [onhz] *adj* eleven
opinyon [ohpinyonh] *n* opinion
opòtinite [ohpotiniteh] *n* opportunity
opoze [opozeh] *v* oppose
opoze [opozeh] *adj* against

oral [ohral] *adj* oral, recited

oranj [oranhj] *adj* orange

orè [oerh] *n* schedule

orijin [orijhin] *n* origin

osinon [ohsinonh] *conj* else

osinon [ohseenonh] *conj* or else

ositou [oseetwo] *adv* also

ospitalite [ospitaliteh] *n* hospitality

oswa [oswa] *conj* either

otan [otanh] *prp* so, so much; stop! enough

otè [oteh] *n* author; height

otès [otess] *n* hostess

otobis [ohtobis] *n* bus

otorize [ohtoreezeh] *v* authorize, allow;
   empower

otou [ohtou] *adv* surrounding, around

ou [woo] *prn* you, your

ou-menm [woo-menhm] *prn* yourself

out [oot] *n* August

ouvri [oovree] *v* open, extend

ouvriye [ouvriyeh] *n* worker

P

pa   [pah] *n* step
padonnen   [pahdonhnenh] *v* forgive
padsi   [padsee] *n* overcoat
pafen   [pafenh] *n* perfume
Pak   [pak] *n* Easter
pake   [pakeh] *n* bundle, pack, parcel
pal   [pal] *adj* dim, faint, pale
pale   [pahlayh] *v* speak
palè   [paleh] *n* palace
palmante   [palmanhteh] *v* parley
palmis   [palmiss] *n* palmtree
pami   [pamee] *prp* among
pàn   [pahn] *n* malfunction
panche   [panhsheh] *v* lean
pandan   [panhdanh] *prp* during, while
panik   [paneek] *n* panic
panno   [panhno] *n* panel, wall
panse   [panhseh] *v* nurse; *v* think, *n* hought
pant   [panht] *n* slope, inclination
pantalon   [panhtalonh] *n* slacks, trousers,
  pants

pantan [panhtanh] *adj* surprised, taken
  aback, startled

panye [panyeh] *n* basket

papa [papa] *n* father, daddy, *adj* enormous,
  mmense

papiyon [papeeyonh] *n* butterfly, moth, gnat

papye [papyeh] *n* paper

papye twalèt [papyeh twalet] *n* tissue

paradi [pahrahdee] *n* paradise

paralizi [pahrahleezee] *n* palsy

paran [pahranh] *n* parent, relative; family

parapè [parapeh] *n* railing

parazit [pahrahzeet] *n* parasite, vermin

pare [pahreh] *v* ward off, *adj* ready

parese [pahrehseh] *adj* lazy, sluggard

parèt [pareht] *v* appear, come forward

parèy [pahrehy] *adj* alike, similar

pari [paree] *n* bid, bet

paryaj [paryahj] *n* betting

parye [paryeh] *v* bet, wager

pasaje [pahsahjeh] *n* passenger

pase [paseh] *adj* past, last, *v* pass, *adv* go

pasèl [passel] *n* plot

paske [paskeh] *conj* because

pastan [pastanh] *n* leisure

pasyans [pasyanhs] *n* patience

107

pasyon [pahsyonh] *n* passion
pat [pat] *n* dough, batter
pat [pat] *n* paw, hoof
pataje [pahtahjeh] *v* share
patch [patch] *n* patch
patche [patsheh] *v* patch
patè [pateh] *n* landscape
paten [pahtenh] skate
pati [pahtee] *v* leave, go out, travel
patikilye [pahteekeelye] *adj* particular
patisipe [pahtisipeh] participate, partake
patisri [pahtisree] *n* pastry
patnè [patneh] *n* partner; chum
patoje [pahtojeh] *v* wade
patron [patwonh] *n* boss
pave [pahveh] *v* pave
pay [pye] *n* straw
payas [payas] *n* decoy
pè [peh] *n* pair, *adj* double
pè [peh] *adj* afraid, fearful
pè [peh] *n* priest
pèch [pesh] *n* peach
peche [pesheh] *n/v* sin
pedal [pehdahl] *n* pedal
pedale [pehdahleh] *v* pedal
pèdi [pehdee] *v* lose, misguide

pèmanan [pehmananh] *adj* permanent
pèmèt [pehmet] *v* allow, permit
pen [penh] *n* bread, loaf
penetre [pehnehtreh] *v* penetrate, enter
peng [peng] *adj* stingy, selfish
pens [penhs] *n* pliers, pincers
penti [penhti] *n* paint
pentire [penhtireh] *v* paint
peny [penhy] *n* comb
pèp [pep] *n* people
peri [pehri] *v* perish
perime [pehreemeh] *v* lapse
peryòd [pehriod] *n* period, epoch;
   menstruation
pèse [pehseh] *v* pierce
pèsekite [pehsekiteh] *v* persecute
pèsi [pehsee] *n* parsley
pèsiste [pehsisteh] *v* persist
pèsonn [pehson] *prn* nobody
pespektiv [pespektiv] *n* outlook
pèsuade [pessuadeh] *v* persuade
pèt [pet] *n* loss, chagrin; fart
pete [pehteh] explode, burst, explode,
   erupt; fart
peteje [pehtehjeh] *v* blind, dazzle
petèt [pehtet] *adv* perhaps, maybe

petròl   [petwol] *n* petrol
peye   [pehyeh] *v* pay
peyi   [payee] *n* country, *adj* domestic, folk
peyizan   [payeezanh] *n* peasant
peze   [pehzeh] *adj* heavy
peze   [pehzeh] *v* weigh, press; depress; extort
pi...pase   [pee...passe] *adv* more... than
piblisite   [peebliseeteh] *n* advertisement
pibliye   [pibliyeh] *v* publish
pijon   [peejonh] *n* pigeon, dove; penis
pike   [peekeh] *v* prick, *adj* sharp, keen
pil sab   [peel sab] *n* dune
pil fatra   [peel fatra] *n* dump
pil   [peel] *n* heap, pile
pilwen   [peelwenh] *adj* farther
pilye   [peelyeh] pillar
pilye   [peelyeh] *n* column
pimal   [peemal] *adj* worse
piman   [peemanh] *n* pepper
pinèz   [peenez] *n* bug, flea
pini   [peenee] *v* forbid, punish; reprimand
pinisyon   [pinisyonh] *n* punishment
pip   [peep] *n* pipe
pirifye   [pirifyeh] *v* purify
pis   [piss] *n* flea
pisans   [pisanhs] *n* power

pisin [pisin] *n* pool
piti [pitee] *adj* small, little
pitit [piteet] *n* child
pitit gason [piteet gahsonh] *n* son
pito [pito] *adv* rather, *v* prefer
pitye [pityeh] *n* mercy, pity
plafon [plafonh] *n* ceiling
plaj [plahj] *n* beach
plake [plahkeh] *v* affix, *adj* tight
plamen [plahmenh] *n* palm
planch [planch] *n* board
plannen [planhnenh] *v* fly, glide, hover;
  pawn
plant [plant] *n* plant
plantasyon [planhtahsyonh] *n* plantation,
  farm
plas [plas] *n* space; location
plasebo [plahsehbo] *n* placebo
plat [plaht] *n* plate, dish, *adj* flat, shallow
platfòm [platfohm] *n* deck
plato [plahto] *n* tray; valley
plè [pleh] *v* please
plèd [pled] *n* plea
plede [plehdeh] *v* plead, implore
plen [plenh] *adj* full
plenyen [plenhyenh] *v* complain

plezi [plehzee] *n* delight, pleasure
pli [plee] *n* curl, kink, fold
plim [pleem] *n* pen, feather
plis [pliss] *adv* more; plus
plise [pleeseh] *adj* folded, wrinkled
pliye [pleeyeh] *v* fold, bend, curve
plizyè [pleezyeh] *adj* several
plon [plonh] *n* lead
plonje [plonhjeh] *v* dive, dip; sink, plunge
po figi [pofeegee] *n* cheek
po [poh] *n* skin; peel, rind; pot
pò [poh] *n* harbor
pobouch [poboosh] *n* lip
pòch [posh] *n* pocket
poli [pohlee] *adj* polite
pòm [pohm] *n* apple
pòmdetè [pohmdehteh] *n* potato
pon [ponh] *n* bridge, deck
ponp [ponhp] *n* pump
ponpe [ponhpeh] *v* pump; jump, skip
ponyen [ponhyenh] *v* clench, grab
ponyèt [ponhyet] *n* wrist
poro [pohwo] *n* leek
posede [posehdeh] *v* possess, own
posib [pohsib] *adj* possibly
posiblite [pohsibliteh] *n* possibility

pòslèn [poslen] *n* china
poste [pohsteh] *v* mail; post
pòt [pot] *n* door, entrance
pòtay [pottahy] *n* gate
pote dèy [pohtay dey] *v* mourn
pote [pohtay] *v* bring, carry, bear;
pòtè [potteh] *n* porter
poto [poto] *n* pillar, column
pou [poo] *prp* for; louse
poud [pood] *n* powder, *adj* brittle
poukisa [pookisah] *prp* why
poukont [pookont] *adj* alone
poul [pool] *n* chicken
pouli [poolee] *n* pulley
poupe [poopeh] *n* doll, puppet
pouri [pooree] *adj* rotten, addle, decay, *v* rot
pouriti [pooreeti] *n* decay
pous [poohs] *n* thumb; inch
pousantaj [poosanhtaj] *n* percent, rate
pouse [pooseh] *v* push, jog; bump
pouswiv [poosuiv] *v* pursue, follow
pousyè [poosyeh] *n* dust, dirt
pòv [pov] *adj/n* poor
povrete [pohvreteh] *n* poverty
pran [pranh] *v* take, get; obtain
pranpòz [pranpoz] *v* feign

pranswen   [pranhswenh] *v* care, cherish
pratik   [pratik] *adj* convenient; *n* client;
  onvention
preche   [presheh] *v* preach, evangelize
predi   [prehdee] *v* predict
prefas   [prehfas] *n* preface
preferans   [preferans] *n* preference, choice
prefere   [prehfehreh] *v* prefer, favor
prejije   [prehjeejeh] *n* prejudice
prekosyon   [prehkohsyonh] *n* caution,
  precaution
premye   [prehmyeh] *adj* first, initial
prensipal   [prenhsipal] *adj* principal, major
prentan   [prenhtanh] *n* spring
prepare   [prehpareh] *v* prepare
prepare   [prehpahreh] *v* prepare, *adj* ready
prese   [prehseh] *v* hurry, *adj* hurried
presedan   [prehsehdanh] *adj* previous
presede   [prehsehdeh] *v* precede
presi   [prehsee] *adj* exact, precise
presidan   [prehzeedanh] *n* president
prèske   [preskeh] *adv* almost
prèt   [pret] *n* priest
pretann   [prehtan] *v* pretend, allude
prete   [prehteh] *v* borrow; lend, loan
prèv   [prev] *n* proof

114

prevni [prevnee] *v* warn; prevent
prezaj [prezaj] *n* omen
prezan [prehzanh] *adj* present
prezans [prehzanhs] *n* presence
prezante [prehzanhteh] *v* introduce,
  present; propose
prezève [prezehveh] *v* preserve
pri [pree] *n* cost, price
pridan [preedan] *adj* prudent
prim [prim] *n* award
prin [prin] *n* plum
prive [preeveh] *adj* private
priye [preeyeh] *v* pray
priz kouran [preez kooranh] *n* plug
priz [preez] *n* grip
prizon [preezonh] *n* prison
probab [probab] *adj* probable
problem [pwoblem] *n* matter, problem
profesè [pwofehseh] *n* professor
profi [pwofee] *n* profit
profite [pwofeeteh] *v* profit
program [pwogram] *n* program; show
projte [pwojteh] *v* forecast, project
proklame [pwoklahmeh] *v* proclaim
prokreye [pwokreyeh] *v* procreate
rolonje [pwolonhjeh] *v* prolong

promès [pwomess] *n* promise
promèt [pwomet] *v* promise
prononse [pwononhseh] *v* pronounce, voice
pròp [prop] *adj* clean
propoze [pwopozeh] *v* propose
propozisyon [propozeeseeonh] *n* proposal, clause
propriyete [pwopriyeteh] *n* land, holding; property
prosè [pwoseh] *n* process; law suit
prospere [pwospehreh] *v* prosper
proteje [pwotehjeh] *v* protect
proteksyon [pwotekseeonh] *n* protection, cover
prouve [pwooveh] *v* prove
provèb [provehb] *n* proverb
ptiti-pitit [piteet-piteet] *n* grandchild
pui/pi [pee] *n* well
pwa [pwa] *n* bean, pea; weight
pwal [pwal] *n* body hair
pwason [pwahsonh] *n* fish
pwatrin [pwatreen] *n* bosom
pwatrin [pwatrin] *n* chest
pwav [pwav] *n* black pepper
pwazon [pwazonh] *n* poison
pwen [pwenh] *n* point, period; spot; fist

116

pwenti [pwenhti] *adj* acute, sharp
pwenti [pwenhtee] *adj* sharp
pwochen [pwochenh] *adj* next, *n* fellow
  human
pwodui [pwodui] *v* produce, generate
pwofondè [profonhdeh] *n* depth
pwòp [prop] *adj* neat, tidy
pwopriyetè [pwopriyehtay] *n* landlord,
  owner
pwovizyon [pwoveezyonh] *n* grocery,
  provision
pye [pihyeh] *n* foot; leg; tree
pyebwa [pihyehbwa] *n* tree
pyès [pihyes] *n* part, piece
pyese [pihyeseh] *v* mend, patch
pyèsteyat [pihyesteyat] *n* play
pyete [pihyehteh] *v* encroach

Q

R

rach   [rash] *n* axe
rache   [rasheh] *v* uproot, extricate; mince
rad   [rad] *n* clothing; shore
radi   [rahdee] *adj* bold, fresh, insolent,
   impertinent
radyatè   [rahdyateh] *n* radiator
radyografi   [rahdiografee] *n* x-ray
rafal   [rahfahl] *n* gust
rafle   [rahfleh] *v* scrape; miss (target)
rafredi   [rafredee] *v* chill
raj   [rahj] *n* rage
raje   [rahjeh] *n* underbrush, grass, weed
rak   [rack] *n* bush, *adj* acrid
rakbwa   [rakbwa] *n* forest, brush
rakomode   [rahkomodeh] *v* mend, patch
rakonte   [rahkonhteh] *v* narrate, relate, tell
rale   [rahleh] *v* draw, extract, pull, stretch,
   zoom; oan
raliman   [raleemanh] *n* rally
raman   [rahmanh] *adv* rarely
rame   [rahmeh] *v* paddle, row
ranje   [ranhjeh] *n* row

ranje   [ranhjeh] *v* fix, repair; arrange, organize

rankont   [ranhkont] *n* meeting

rankontre   [ranhkontreh] *v* meet

ranmase   [ranhmaseh] *v* find, acquire

ranmase   [ranhmaseh] *v* gather, pick up; fork

rann   [ran] *v* vomit; render

ranni   [ranhnee] *v* howl, roar

ranp   [ranhp] *n* ramp

ranpe   [ranhpeh] *v* crawl, creep, slide

ranpli   [ranhplee] *adj* filled, *v* fulfill

ranse   [ranhsay] *v* dally, joke

ransè   [ranhseh] *n* buffoon

ransi   [ranhsee] *adj* rancid

ranson   [ranhsonh] *n* ransom

rantre   [ranhtreh] *v* enter

ranvwaye   [ranhvwayeh] *v* defer, dismiss; expel

ranyon   [ranhyonh] *n* rag

rapid   [rahpeed] *adj* prompt, rapid, swift

raple   [rahpleh] *v* remind

raproche   [rapwosheh] *v* bring close, *adj* close

rapyese   [rapyehseh] *v* mend, patch

ras kabrit   [rahs kabreet] *adj* inbred

ras   [rahs] *n* race, breed

rasanble [rahsanhbleh] *v* gather, accumulate, collect; ally

rasin [rahsin] *n* root

rasire [rahseereh] *v* reassure

rasmoun [rahsmoon] *n* race

rasyon [rahsyonh] *n* ration

rat [rat] *n* rat

rate [rahteh] *v* fail, miss

ravaj [rahvaj] *n* ravage

ravèt [ravet] *n* roach

ravin [rahvin] *n* ditch, pit

rayi [rahee] *v* hate, detest, abhor

rayisman [raheesmanh] *n* hatred

raz [raz] *adj* boring

raz [raz] *adj* boring, vague

raze [rahze] *v* shave; maneuver closely

razwa [razwa] *n* razor, *adv* boring

razya [razya] *n* raid

rebelyon [rehbehlyonh] *n* rebellion

rebò [reboh] *n* brim, contour

rèd [red] *adj* tough, rigid, tense

redui [redui] *v* reduce

refere refer refize

[rehfeezeh] *v* refuse, decline

reflechi [reflechee] *v* reflect, think, ponder

règ [reg] *n* rule; period
rega [rehgah] *n* look
regrèt [rehgret] *v* regret
rejè [rehjeh] *n* reject
rejete [rehjehteh] *v* reject; throw up
rejwi [rejwee] rejoice, enjoy
rejyon [rehjyonh] *n* region, zone
reklam [rehklam *n* advertisement
reklamasyon [reklamaseeonh] *n* claim
rekòlt [rehkolt] *n* crop, harvest
rekòlte [rehkolteh] *v* harvest
rekòmande [rehkomanhdeh] recommend,
  urge
rekonesans [rehkohnehsanhs] *n* gratitude
rekonèt [rehkohnet[*v* recognize
rekonfòte [rekonhfoteh] *v* comfort
rekoni [rehkohni] *adj* known, popular
rekonpans [rehkonhpanhs] *n* reward
rekreyasyon [rehkrehyasyonh] *n* recreation,
  recess
rekrite [rekriteh] *v* enroll, recruit
relate [relahteh] *v* describe, recount, relate
rele [rehleh] *v* call; name; scream, shout,
  yell
relijyez [rehlijyez] *n/adj* nun, religious
relye [rehlyeh] *v* link

remak   [rehmak] *n* remark

remake   [rehmahkeh] *v* mention, remark

remèd   [rehmed] *n* medication, remedy

remèsye   [rehmehsyeh] *v* thank

remèt   [rehmet] *v* remit, return, render;
   submit

remò   [remoh] *n* remorse

ren   [renh] *n* kidney; waist; middle

rèn   [rehn] *n* queen

renmen   [renhmenh] *v* like, love

rennen   [renhnenh] *v* constrain

rense   [renhseh] *v* rinse

renye   [rehnyeh] *v* deny

repase   [rehpahseh] *v* review; iron

repati   [rehpatee] *v* allot

repete   {rehpehteh] *v* repeat; pronounced,
   prominent

reponn   [rehpon] *v* answer, respond

repons   [rehponhs] *n* answer, response

repoze   [rehpohzeh] *v* rest

repran   [rehpranh] *v* recover

reprimande   [repreemanhdeh] *v* reprimand,
   castigate

reprize   [rehpreezeh] *v* sew, repair

resan   [rehsanh] *adj* recent, up-to-date

resevwa   [rehsevwa] *v* receive; host

resipwòk [rehsipwok] *adj* mutual

resò [rehsoh] *n* spring

respè [rehspeh] *n* respect

respekte [respekteh] *v* respect, abide

respire [rehspeereh] *v* breathe

restan [rehstanh] *n* remainder, rest

restavèk [restavek] *n* domestic, maid, servant

restrenn [rehstren] *v* restrict

retade [rehtahdeh] *v* delay, postpone

rete [rehteh] *v* stay; live, inhabit

retire [rehteereh] *v* remove, eject, exclude; withdraw

retresi [rehtrehsee] *v* shrink

rèv [rev] *n* dream

revandike [rehvanhdeekeh] *v* assert, claim

revanj [rehvanhj] *n* revenge

revele [rehvehleh] *v* reveal

revèy [rehvehy] *n* clock

reveye [rehvehyeh] *v* wake up, *adj* awake

revi [rehvee] *n* magazine, review

revoke [rehvokeh] *v* fire, revoke, impeach

revolvè [rehvolveh] *n* hand gun

reyalizasyon [rehyahleezasyonh] *n* attainment

reyalize [rehyahleezeh] *v* achieve

reyèl [rehyel] *adj* real

reyini [rayini] *v* convene, congregate, *adj* eunited

reyisi [reyeesee] *v* achieve, succeed, flourish

reyon [rehyonh] *n* beam, ray

rezen [rehzenh] *n* grape

rezilta [rehzeelta] *n* outcome

reziste [rehzisteh] *v* resist, withstand

rezon [rezonh] *n* reason, cause

rezoud [rehzood] *v* solve

ri [ree] *v* laugh; street

riban [reebanh] *n* ribbon, band

rich [reesh] *adj* rich

richès [reeshess] *n* fortune

rid [reed] *n* wrinkle

rido [reedo] *n* curtain

rijid [reejeed] *adj* rigid

rilaks [reelaks] *adj/v* relax

risk [risk] *n* risk

riske [riskeh] *v* risk, venture

rivaj [reevaj] *n* coast

rive [reeveh] *v* arrive, befall, happen, occur; prosper

rivyè [reevyeh] *n* creek, stream

rize [reezeh] *adj* astute, crafty, sly

ro {wo} [woh] *adj* tall; high

ròb {wòb}   [rob] *n* dress
ròch   [wosh] *n* stone, rock
rode   [rohdeh] *v* prowl
ròl   [rol] *n* role
roman   [wohmanh] *n* novel
romans   [wohmanhs] *n* romance
ron {won}   [wonh] *adj* round
ronfle   [wonhfleh] *v* snore
ronm   [wonhm] *n* rum
ront   [wont] *adj* ashamed, *n* shame, *v* blush
rote   [wohteh] *v* belch
rou {wou}   [woo] *n* wheel
rouj {wouj}   [wooj] *adj* red
rouji   [woojee] *v*redden
roule   [wooleh] *v* roll
roulib   [woolib] *n* lift, ride
roulo   [wooloh] *n* roll
rousi   [woosee] *v* burn, sear
rout {wout}   [woot] *n* route
rouy   [wooy] *n* rust
rouye   [wooyeh] *v* rust, corrode, *adj* rusty
roz   [wohz] *n* rose, *adj* pink
ruin   [win] *n* ruin
ruine   [winheh] *v* ruin

S

sab   [sab] *n* sand

sachè   [sahsheh] *n* bag

saj   [sahj] *adj* wise

sak   [sack] *n* sack

sal   [sahl] *adj* dirty, filthy, *v* soil

salad   [sahlad] *n* salad

sale   [salay] *adj* salty, *v* season with salt

salè   [saleh] *n* income, salary

salte   [salteh] *n* dirt, grime

salye   [sahlyeh] *v* salute, greet

samdi   [samdee] *n* Saturday

san   [sanh] *prp* without, *n* blood, *adj* undred

sanble   [sanhbleh] *v* seem, appear; *adj* similar

sandriye   [sanhdriyeh] *n* ashtray

sandwich   [sanhdwish] *n* sandwich

sann   [sann] *n* cinder

sanpitye   [sanhpityeh] *adj* pitiless, callous

sans   [sanhs[*n* sense, meaning

sansib   [sanhsib] *adj* sensible; sensitive, tender

sant   [sanht] *n* scent, smell; *n* centre

sante   [sanhteh] *n* health

santi   [sanhtee] *v* feel; smell, *adj* reek, stench

sanzatann   [sanhzatan] *adv* suddenly, *adj* freak

sanzave   [sanhzaveh] *n* ragamuffin

satire   [sahteereh] *v* saturate

satisfè   [satisfeh] *v* satisfy

savann   [sahvan] *n* savanna

save   [sahveh] *n* knowledge

savon   [sahvonh] *n* soap

savonnen   [sahvonhnenh] *v* soap

sè   [seh] *n* sister

sechrès   [seshress] *n* drought

sede   [sehdeh] *v* concede, give up

sedui   [sehdui] *v* seduce

segonde   [sehgonhdeh] *v* aid, help, assist ; second

segonn   [segon] *n* second

sèk   [sek] *adj* dry, brittle, crisp, *n* circle

sekans   [sehkans] *n* sequence

sèkèy   [sehkey] *n* coffin

sekrè   [sehkreh] *n* secret

sèks   [sex] *n* gender; sex

sèl   [sel] *n* salt; harness, *adj* alone, lone

sele   [seleh] *v* harness; seal; secure

selebre [selebreh] *v* celebrate

seleksyone [seleksyoneh] *v* select, chose

selibatè [selibahteh] *adj* single, *n* bachelor

sèlman [selmanh] *adv* only, merely

selon lizaj [sehlonh leezahj] *adj* usual

sèman [sehmanh] *n* oath

semèn {senmenn} [sehmehn] *n* week

sen [senh] *adj* holy, *n* saint

sendika [sendeeka] *n* union

senesòf [senhnehsof] *adj* safe

senk [senhk] *adj* five

senkant [senhkanht] *adj* fifty

senp [senhp] *adj* simple

sensè [senhseh] *adj* sincere

senti [senhtee] *n* waist

sentiron [senhteewonh] *n* belt, sash

senyen [senhyenh] *v* bleed

separe [sepahreh] *v* separate, break

separe [saypareh] *adj* detached *v* share, split

separe [sehpareh] *v* divide, *adj* divided

septanm [septanhm] *n* September

sere [sehreh] *adj* tight, *v* hide; hug; tighten

sereng [sehrenhg] *n* syringe

sereyal [sehreyahl] *n* cereal

seriz [sehreez] *n* cherry

serye [sehryeh] *adj* serious, vital

sèt [set] *adj* seven
sèten [sehtenh] *adj* certain, sure
sètènman [sehtehnmanh] *adv* certainly
sètifye [setifyeh] *v* certify
sevè [sehveh] *adj* severe
sèvi [sehvee] *v* serve
sèvis [sehvis] *n* service
sèvo [sehvo] *n* brain
sèvolan [sehvolanh] *n* kite
sèvyèt [sehvyet] *n* towel, napkin
sezi [sehzee] *v* seize
si [see] *adj* sure; sour, *conj* if
sibi [seebee] *v* suffer, undergo
sid [seed] *n* south
sifizan [sifizanh] *adj* sufficient
siflèt/souflèt [seeflet] *n* whistle
sijè [seejeh] *n* subject
sijere [seejehreh] *v* suggest
sik [sik] *n* sugar
sikisal [sikisal] *n* outlet
sikonstans [sikonhstanhs] *n* circumstance
sikre [seekreh] *adj* sweet
siksè [seekseh] *n* success
silab [seelab] *n* syllable
silans [seelanhs] *n* silence
silèks [seeleks] *n* flint

silvouple [seelvoopleh] *interj* please
siman [seemanh] *n* concrete, *adv* surely
simen [seemenh] *v* sow
simityè [seemityeh] *n* cemetery
sinema [seenehma] *n* cinema
sinonim [seenonim] *n* synonym
siperyè [sipehryeh] *adj* superior
sipliye [sipliyeh] *v* beseech, beg, yearn
sipò [sipoh] *n* support, aid
sipòte [seepohteh] *v* endure; support; withstand
sipoze [sipohzeh] *v* suppose, assume
sipozisyon [seepohzeesionh] *n* supposition
siprann [seepran] *v* surprise, astonish
sipriz [seepriz] *n* surprise
sirèt [siret] *n* confectionery, candy
sirk [seerk] *n* circus
sirote [sirohteh] *v* sip
sis [sis] *adj* six
sispann [seespan] *v* stop, adjourn, cease
sispèk [sispek] *n/adj* suspect
siswafè [seeswafeh] *adj* certain; knowlegeable
sitèlman [seetelmanh] *adv* so much
sitron [seetwonh] *n* lemon

131

siveyans [sivehyanhs] *n* custody, confinement

siveye [seevehyeh] *v* guard, watch

siviv [seeviv] *v* survive

siy [seey] *n* sign

siyati [seeyatee] *n* signature

siye [seeyeh] *v* wipe

siyen [seeyenh] *v* sign

sizo [seezo] *n* scissors

skilte [skeelteh] *v* carve

sò [soh] *n* fate

sòf [sof] *prp* barring, except

solanèl [sohlahnel] *adj* solemn

solda [soldah] *n* soldier

solèy {sole} [sohlehy] *n* sun

solid [sohleed] *adj* solid; strong *n* solid

solisyon [sohleesyonh] *n* solution

somon [sohmonh] *n* salmon

son [sonh] *n* sound

sonje [sonhjeh] *v* remember

sonm [sonhm] *adj* somber, dreary

sonnen [sohnenh] *v* ring, blow

sòs [sauce] *n* sauce, gravy

sosis [sohsis] *n* sausage

sòsye [sossyeh] *n* wizard

sosyete [sosyeteh] *n* society

soti [sohtee] *v* go out, leave
sou [soo] *prp* onto, *adj* drunk
soud [sood] *adj* deaf
souf [souf] *n* breath
soufle [soofleh] *v* blow, fan; puff
souflete [sooflehteh] *v* slap
soufri [soofree] *v* ail, suffer
souke [sookeh] *v* shake
soukote [sookohteh] *n* illegitimate
soukoup [sookoop] *n* saucer
soulaje [soolajeh] *v* allay, alleviate
soulajman [soolahjmanh] *n* relief
soulye [soolyeh] *n* shoe
soumèt [soomet] *v* submit
sounwa [soonwa] *adj* sly
soup [soup] *n* soup
soupl [soopl] *adj* supple, gentle
souple [soopleh] *interj* please
souri [sooree] *v* smile
sourit [soorit] *n* mouse
sous [soos] *n* source; brook
souse [sooseh] *v* suck; leak
sousi [soosee] *n* eyebrow
souskri [sooskree] *v* subscribe
sousòl [soosol] *n* basement

soutèt [sewtet] *prp* above
soutèt [souteht] *adv* atop
soutni [sootnee] *v* uphold; collaborate
souvan [soovsnh] *adv* often
sovaj [sovaj] *adj* savage; brute, wild
sove [sohvay] *v* save; escape, evade
sovè [sohveh] *n* savior
spektak [spektak] *n* spectacle; program
spesifik [spesifik] *adj* specific, peculiar
stasyon [stahsyonh] *n* station
stat [stat] *v* start
strik [strik] *adj* strict
sue {swe} [sueh] *v* sweat
suiv [suiv] *v* follow, track
swa [swa] *n* silk, *adj* sleek. *n* evening, usk
swanye {swayeh} [swahnyeh] *v* cure
sware [swareh] *n* evening
swasanndis [swasandees] *adj* seventy
swen [swenh] *n* care
swete [sweteh] *v* wish
switch [switch] *n* switch
syans [siyanhs] *n* science
syèk [siyehk] *n* century
syèl [siyel] *n* sky, paradise, heaven

T

ta [tah] *adj* late, overdue

tab [tab] *n* table

tabli [tablee] *adj* settled

taboure [tabooreh] *n* stool

tach [tash] *n* dot, spot, blot

tache [tasheh] *v* stain; bind, attach, fasten, pin

taks [tax] *n* duty, tax

taksi [taxi] *n* taxicab

talan [tahlanh] *n* knack. skill

talè [taheh] *adv* soon

talon [tahlonh] *n* heel

tan [tanh] *n* time; weather

tankou [tanhkoo] *adj* alike; *adv* as

tann [tan] *adj* tender, sensitive

tann [tan] *v* wait

tanp [tanhp] *n* temple

tanperaman [tanhpehramanh] *n* temper

tanpèt [tanhpet] *n* tempest

tanpon [tanhponh] *n* seal

tansfè [tranhsfeh] *n* transfer

tansyon [tanhsyonh] *n* stress, tension

135

tant   [tanht] *n* aunt; tent

tantatif   [tanhtahtif] *n* attempt

tante   [tanhteh] *v* entice, tempt

tape   [tahpeh] *v* tap

tapi   [tahpee] *n* carpet

tat   [taht] *n* pie

tate   [tahteh] *v* finger

tay   [tahy] *n* waist

tayè   [tahyeh] *n* tailor

tcheke   [tshekeh] *v* gauge; ascertain

tchwi   [chwi] *n* leather

te   [teh] *n* tea

tè   [teh] *n* earth, land

tèl   [tell] *adj* such

tèm   [tehm] *n* term

temerè   [temereh] *adj* bold

temwen   [tehmwenh] *n/v* witness

tenbre   [tehnbreh] *v* stamp

tenèb   [tehneb] *n* gloom, obscurity

tenm   [tehnm] *n* stamp

tep   [tehp] *n* scotch tape; cassette
  tape/player; tip

teren   [tehrenh] *n* plot, terrain, field; ground

terib   [tehreeb] *adj* terrible, fierce

terifyan   [tehrifyanh] *adj* appalling, awful

terifye   [terifyeh] *v* terrify, scare

tès [tess] *n* egzam, *n/v* test
tèt [tet] *n* head; brain. *n* self
tèt [tet] *n* head; top; self;
tètchaje [tètchajeh] *n* disarray
tete [tehteh] *n* breast, *v* breastfeed
tètkay [tètkahy] *n* roof
tibèf [teebef] *n* calf
tifi [teefee] *n* girl, daughter; *adj* virgin, haste
tigason [teegasonh] *n* boy, little boy
tikè [teekeh] *n* ticket
timid [timid] *adj* shy, timid
timoun [teemoon] *n* baby, infant; child, kid
tinedjè [teenedjeh] *n* teenager
tinen [teenenh] *n* dwarf
tire [teereh] *v* shoot
tirè [teereh] *n* hyphentise [tisseh] *v* weave
tit [tit] *n* title
titile [teeteeleh] *v* keep up
tiye {touye} [teeyeh] *v* kill
tiyo [teeyo] *n* pipe
tòch [tosh] *n* torch, wipe
tòchonnen [toshonenh] *v* trash, mess up
tòde {tòdye} *v* twist, wring
tomat [tomat] *n* tomato
tonbe [tonhbeh] *v* fall

tonm   [tonhm] *n* grave, tomb
tonnèl   [tonel] *n* shelter
tonton   [tonhtonh] *n* uncle
toro   [toro] *n* bull, *adj* important, strong
total   [total] *adj* total; complete
tòti   [tottee] *n* tortoise
tou   [two] *adv* also; too
toubiyon   [toobeeyonh] *n* whirl
touche   [tousheh] *v* touch, affect; collect
touf   [toof] *n* clump
toufe   [toofeh] *v* choke, strangle, quash, *adj* teamed
toujou   [toojoo] *adv* always
toulede   [toolehdeh] *adj* both
toulejou   [toolehjoo] *adj* daily
toumante   [toomanhteh] *v* torment, tease
tounen   [toonenh] return; turn around; become
toupiti   [toopiti] *adv* slightly, *adj* tiny
toupize   [toopizee] *v* squeeze, mistreat
toupre   [toopreh] *adv* close, near
tous   [toos] *n* cough
touse   [tooseh] *v* cough
tout   [toot] *adj* all, entire
toutan   [tootanh] *adv* always
toutbon   [tootbonh] *adj* real

138

toutouni   [tootoonee] *adj* bare, naked, nude
tradui   [tradui] *v* translate
trafik   [traffic] *n* traffic
traka   [trahkah] *n* trouble, worry
trakase   [trahkahseh] *v* harass, torment,
  worry
tranble   [tranhbleh] *v* tremble, shiver
tranblemantè   [tranhblehmanhteh] *n* quake
tranch   [tranhsh] *n* slice
tranche   [tranhsheh] *v* slice, *n* labor pains
trangle   [tranhgleh] *v* strangle
trankil   [tranhkeel] *adj* quiet, placid
tranpe   [trenhpeh] *v* quench, soak, *n* mixture
tranpe   [tranhpeh] *v* soak; *n* solution, blend,
  oncoction
transfere   [tranhsfehreh] *v* transfer
transmèt   [tranhsmet] *v* convey
transparan   [tranhsparanh] *adj* transparent
trant   [tranht] *adj* thirty
trase   [trahseh] *v* trace
travay   [trahvahy] *v/n* work, task, employ
travayè   [travayeh] *n* worker
travèse   [travehseh] *v* cross, traverse
trayi   [trahyee] *v* betray
tren   [trenh] *n* train; noise
trennen   [trenhnenh] *v* drag, lug

tresayi [tresahyee] *v* cringe
trese [trehseh] *v* braid
trèt [tret] *n* traitor
trete [trehteh] *v* treat
tretman [tretmanh] *n* cure
trèz [trehz] *adj* thirteen
trezò [trehzoh] *n* treasure
tribinal [tribeenal] *n* court, tribunal
trikote [treekoteh] *v* knit
trimen [treemenh] *v* toil
tripotay [treepohtaj] *n* gossip
tripote [treepohteh] *v* finger
tris [triss] *adj* sad, dreary; unhappy
trò [twoh] *adv* too
tròk {twòk} [twok] *n* barter, exchange
troke [twokeh] *v* barter
tronpe [twonhpeh] cheat, deceive, fool
trou [twoo] *n* hole, pit; cavity
trouble [twoobleh] *v* trouble, upset; affect
troup [twoop] *n* troup, flock
trouve [trooveh] *v* find
twa [twah] *adj* three
twakay [twakahy] *n* roof
twal [twahl] *n* cloth; canvas
twalèt [twalet] *n* bathroom; ablution
twou [twoo] *n* ditch, hole

twounen   [twoonenh] *n* nostril
tyèd   [tyehd] *adj* warm

U

uit [uit] *adj* eight

V

vach [vash] *n* cow
vag [vag] *adj* vague, lax, negligent, *n* wave
vakabon [vakahbonh] *n* drifter, vagabond,
  adj naughty
vakans [vahkanhs] *n* vacation
vale [vahlay] *v* swallow, gulp
valè [vahleh] *n* value, worth
valiz [vahleez] *n* valise, suitcase
valv [valve] *n* valve
van [vanh] *n* wind, storm
vandredi [vanhdredi] *n* Friday
vaniy [vaneey] *n* vanilla
vanje [vanhjeh] *v* avenge
vann [van] *v* sell, peddle
vant [vanht] *n* stomach, belly
vante [vanhteh] *v* fan; boast, brag
vantilatè [vanhtilateh] *n* fan
vanyan [vanhyanh] *adj* valiant
vapè [vahpeh] *n* vapor, steam; fume
varye [vahryeh] *v* vary, *adj* spoiled
vast [vast] *adj* vast

vè [veh] *n* glass; worm; verse, *adj* {vèt}
  green
vèf [vehf] *n* widower
vekse [vehkseh] *v* vex, *adj* vexed
vèmin [vehmin] *n* vermin
ven [venh] *adj* twenty
venere [vehnehreh] *v* venerate, respect
vèni [vehnee] *n/v* varnish
venk [vank] *v* defeat, vanquish; overcome
verifye [vereefyeh] *v* verify, prove; audit;
  check
verite [vehriteh] *n* truth
vès [vehs] *n* vest; cardigan
vètikal [veteekal] *adj* vretical
vèv [vehv] *n* widow
veye [vehyeh] *n* wake; *v* watch
vi [vee] *n* life
vid [veed] *adj* empty; blank
vide [veedeh] *v* pour; discharge; flush;
  empty
viktim [victeem] *n/adj* victim
viktwa [victwa] *n* victory
vil [veal] *n* city, town
vilaj [veelahj] *n* village
vinèg [venehg] *n* vinegar
vini [veenee] *v* come; become

144

vire   [veereh] *v* turn

vis   [vis] *n* vice; screw

visye   [veesye] *adj* greedy

vit   [veet] *n* glass; *adj* fast, quick, rapid

vital   [veetal] *adj* vital, serious

vitès   [veetess] *n* speed

viv   [veev] *v* live; inhabit; occupy

vivan   [veevanh] *adj* alive

vize   [vizeh] *v* aim target

vizyon   [veezyonh] *n* vision, premonition

vle   [vleh] *v* want

vlope   [vlohpeh] *v* wrap

vokabilè   [vohkabeeleh] *n* vocabulary

vòl   [vol] *n* flight; theft

volay   [vohlahy] *n* fowl

vole, tronpe cheat *v*   vole, vòlè steal

vole {vòlè}   [vohlay] *v* fly, jump; steal; cheat

vòlè   [vohleh] *n* thief, rascal, rogue

vòlè   [volleh] *n* crook, robber, thief; *adj* greedy

volim   [vohleem] *n* volume

volonte   [vohlonhtay] *n* will

volontè   [vohlonhteh] *n* volunteer

vomi   [vohmee] *n/v* vomit, throw up; puke

voryen   [voryenh] *n* buffoon, rascal. scamp

vòt   [vot] *n* ballot, vote

145

vote   [vohteh] *v* vote

voye   [voyeh] *v* cast, throw, send; broadcast; ejaculate

vre   [vreh] *adj* true

vwa   [vwah] *n* voice

vwal   [vwahl] *n* sail

vwayaj   [vwayaj] *n* travel, trip, voyage; journey

vwayaje   [vwayajeh] *v* travel

vwazen   [vwazwnh] *n* neighbor

vyann   [veeyan] *n* meat; flesh

vye   [vyeh] *adj* old, ancient, bad

vyèj   [vyehj] *adj* virgin

vyèyfi   [vyehyfee] *n* spinster

vyeyi   [vyehi] *v* age, *adj* aged, elder

vyole   [vyoleh] *v* rape, ravish; violate

vyolèt   [vyohlet] *adj* violet

W

wa [wah] *n* king
waf [waf] *n* wharf, harbor
wè [weh] *v* see
wi [wee] *adv* yes
wiski [weeskee] *n* whisky
wo [woe] *adj* high; elevated
wont [wont] *n* shame, disgrace
wotè [woeteh] *n* height

X

Y

yenyen   [yenhyenh] *adj* whimpering
yè   [yeh] *n* yesterday
yo   [yoh] *prn* they
yòd {tentidyòd}   [yod] *n* iodine
yota   [yotah] *n* iota
youn   [yoon] *adj* one

Z

zak   [zak] *n* act
zam   [zahm] *n* weapon
zandolit   [zanhdoleet] *n* lizard
zangi   [zanhgee] *n* eel
zanmi   [zanhmee] *n* friend; acquaintance;
   chum
zannimo   [zanhimoh] *n* animal
zanno   [zanhno] *n* earring
zantray   [zanhtrahy] *n* entrails, gut(s)
zariyen   [zahrenhyenh] *n* spider
ze   [zeh] *n* egg
zèb   [zeb] *n* grass, hay
zegi   [zehgee] *n* needle
zeklè   [zehkleh] *n* lightning
zen   [zenh] *n* hook
zenk   [zenhk] *n* zinc
zepeng   [zehpenhg] *n* pin
zepis   [zehpiss] *n* spice, herbs
zepòl   [zehpol] *n* shoulder
zetwal   [zetwal] *n* star
zèv   [zehv] *n* charity
zigzag   [zigzag] *n* zigzag

zigzage [zigzageh] *v* zigzag
zile [zeeleh] *n* island
zilofòn [zeelofon] *n* xylophone
zip [zip] *n* zipper
zipe [zipeh] *v* zip
zo [zoh] *n* bone
zokòt [zohkot] *n* rib
zòn [zohn] *n* zone, region
zonbi [zonhbee] *n* zombie, ghost
zong [zonhg] *n* nail
zongle [zonhgleh] *v* pinch; nip
zonyon [zonhyonh] *n* onion
zoranj [zohranj] *n* orange
zòrèy [zohrehy] *n* ear
zorye [zohryeh] *n* pillow
zòtèy [zohtehy] *n* toe
zou [zoo] *n* zoo
zouti [zootee] *n* tool
zuit [zuit] *n* oyster
zwa [zwah] *n* goose
zwazo [zwazo] *n* bird
zye [zyeh] *n* eye

ENGLISH-CREOLE

A

aback   [ebak] *adv* pa sipriz
abandon   [abendenn] *v* abandone, kite
abase   [ebes] *v* abese, diminye
abash   [ebach] *v* demoralize
abbreviate   [aebrivyet] *v* abreje
abdicate   [abdiket] *v* abdike
abduct   [abdòkt] *v* kidnape, anlve
abet   [ebèt] *v* ensite, eksite
abhor   [aebhòr] *v* deteste, rayi
abide   [aebayd] *v* respekte
ability   [aebiliti] *n* abilite, aptitud
abject   [abdjèkt] *adj* abjèk, degoutan
able   [ebl] *adj* kapab
abolish   [abolich] *v* aboli
abound   [ebawnd] *v* gen anpil, abonde
about   [aebawt] *prp* apropo
above   [aebòv] *prp* anlè, soutèt
abrade   [aebreid] *v* graje, fwote, kòche
abreast   [aebrèst] *adv* okouran
abridge   [aebridj] *v* abreje
abroad   [aebròd] *adv* lòtbò

abrupt   [aebròpt] *adj* abrip, brid sou kou, bripbrip

absence   [apsans] *n* absans

absolve   [apsòlv] *v* absoud

absorb   [apzoòb] *v* absòbe

abstain   [apsten]*v* abstrenn

absurd   [apsèad] *adj* absid

abuse   [abyouz] *n* abi, *v* abize

accede   [aksid] *v* aksede, rantre

accept   [aksèpt] *v* aksepte

access   [aksès] *n* aksè, *v* aksede, rantre

accident   [aksident] *n* aksidan

accommodate   [akomodet] *v* akomode, loje

accomplish   [aekonmplich] *v* akonpli

accord   aekoòd] *n* akò, *v* akòde

accost   [aekòst] *v* akoste, bòde

account   [aekawnt] *n* kont, *v* jistifye, eksplike

accumulate   [aekyumyulet] *v* akimile, rasanble

accurate   [aekyuret] *adj* egzak, byen mezire (konte)

accustom   [aekòstonm] *v* familyarize

ache   [eik] *n* doulè, mal

achieve   [aetchiv] *v* reyalize, reyisi

acquaint   [aekwent] *v* fè konesans

acquaintance   [aekwenntanns]*n* konesans, zanmi

acquire   [aekwayèu] *v* ranmase, trouve

acquit   [aekwit] *v* akite

acrid   [akrid] *adj* rak, brak

across   [aekròs] *adv* atravè

act   [akt] *v* aji, *n* zak, akt

actuate   [aktuet] *v* balanse, aksyonen

acute   [akyout] *adj* pwenti, egu

adapt   [adapt] *v* adapte

add   [ad] *v* adisyone, ajoute, ogmante

addict   [adikt] *adj* droge, adikte

addle   [adl] *adj* pouri

address   [adrès] *n* adrès

adequate   [adekwet] *adj* adekwa, sifizan

adjective   [adjektiv] *n* adjektif

adjourn   [adjòrn] *v* ajoune, sispann

adjust   [adjòst] *v* ajiste

admire   [admayèu] *v* admire

admirer   [admayrèu] *n* admiratè, fanatik

admit   [admit] *v* admèt, aksepte

admonish   [admonich] *v* joure, avèti

adolescent   [adolèsant] *n* adolesan

adopt   [adòpt] *v* adopte

adore   [aedòr] *v* adore

adorn   [adòrn] *v* òne, dekore

adult   [adòlt] *n* adilt, granmoun

advance   [advenns] *n* avans, avalwa *v*
  avanse, bay avalwa

advantage   [advenntedj] *n* avantaj

adventure   [advenntyèu] *n* risk, istwa dròl

advertisement   [advèutayzment] *n* reklam,
  piblisite

advice   [advays] *n* konsèy

affable   [aefebl] *adj* afab

affair   [aefèr] *n* afè, kesyon, lyezon

affect   [aefèkt] *v* afekte, touche, trouble

affirm   [aefèum] *v* afime, deklare

affix   [aefiks] *v* afiche, plake

afford   [aefòrd] *v* gen (jwenn) mwayen

affront   [aefront] *n* afron *v* afronte

afoot   [aefout] *adv* apye

afraid   [aefreid] *adj* pè, efreye

afresh   [aefrèch] *adj* ankò, a nouvo

after   [aftèu] *adv* apre, dèyè

again   [aegen] *adv* ankò

against   [aegenst] *adv* kont, opoze

age   [edj] *n* laj, *v* vyeyi

agile   [adjayl] *adj* ajil, lèst

ago   [aego] *adj* pase, *adv* depi

agree   [aegrii] *v* konsanti, dakò

ahead   [aehèd] *adj* devan

aid [aeid] *n* èd, sipò
ail [aeil] *v* soufri
aim [aeim] *n* bi, *v* vize
air [aeir] *n* lè
ale [ael] *n* byè
alert [aelèut] *adj* sou kiviv, eveye
alien [aelyenn] *n* etranje
alike [aelayk] *adj* tankou, menm, parèy
aliment [aelimennt] *n* manje
alive [aelayv] *adj* vivan
all [òwl] *adj* tout
allay [aley] *v* soulaje, diminye
allot [aelòt] *v* repati, lote
allow [aelaw] *v* pèmèt, otorize
allude [alyoud] *v* pretann, sipoze
allure [alyur] *n* atire
allusion [aluzyonn] *n* alizyon, sipozisyon
ally [alay] *n* alye
almost [òlmost] *adv* prèske, prèt pou
alone [aelon] *adj* (pron.) sèl, pou
kont-(pron.)
along [aelonng] *adj* ansanm
aloof [aelouf] *adj* endiferan, lwen
aloud [aelawd] *adv* aotvwa, byen fò
already [òlrwedi] *adv* deja
also [òlso] *adv* tou, ositou

158

alter [altèu] *v* chanje, altere
although [òldvo] *adv* malgre
always [òlwez] *adv* toujou, tout tan
amateur [amatèu] *n* amatè
amazing [aemezing] *adj* etonan
ambassador [enmbasadòr] *n* anbasadè
amber [aembèu] *adj* oranj, abriko
amend [amennd] *v* korije
amenity [ameniti] *n* konfò, amenajman
amiable [amyebl] *adj* emab
among [aemong] *prp* pami, omilyc
amount [aemawnt] *n* montan, total
ample [anmpl] *adj* ase, gran, laj, sifi(zan)
amuse [aemyouz] *v* amize
ancient [annsyent] *adj* ansyen, vye
and [ennd] *conj* ak, epi, e
anew [aenyou] *adv* ankò, anouvo
anger [anngèu] *n* kòlè *v* (fè) fache
angle [aenngèul] *n* angl, aspè
angry [aenngri] *adj* fache
animal [animal] *n* animal, zannimo
anniversary [aenivèusèuri] *n* fèt, anivèsè
announce [aenawns] *v* anonse
annoy [aenòy] *v* anniye, anmède
annual [anuyòl *adj* anyèl, chak ane, lan
another [ennòdvèu] *adj/prn* onlòt

answer [ennsèu] *n* repons, *v* reponn
ant [ent] *n* foumi
anxiety [enkzayti] *n* enkyetid, anksyete
any [eni] *adj* nenpòt
apart [aepart] *adv* aleka, separe, detache
apologize [aepolodjayz] *v* e(k)skize
appall [aepal] *v* efarouche, terifye
appalling [aepaling] *adj* terifyan
appeal [aepil] *n* JUR. fè apèl, cham
appear [aepir] *v* gen lè, parèt, sanble
append [aepennd] *v* tahce, kole, ajoute
appendix [aepenndiks] *n* apendis
apple [apèul] *n* pòm (frans)
appoint [aepòynt] *v* nonmen, dezinyen
appraise [aeprez] *v* evalue, estime
appreciate [aeprichyet] *v* apresye
apprehend [aeprihennd] *v* apreyande, arete
approach [aeprotch] *v* aproche, *n* aksè,
    FIG. apròch, fason
approve [aeprouv] *v* aprouve
approximate [aeproksimet] *adj*
    aproksimatif, *v* aproksime
apricot [aeprikòt] *n* (z)abriko
April [aepril] *n* avril
apt [apt] *adj* jis, apropriye
archbishop [aèkbichòp] *n* monsenyè

argue   [aègyou] *v* diskite, mentni
arise   [aerayz] *v* pete, gaye, provni
arm   [aèm] *n* bra, *v* ame
armchair   [amtchèr] *n* fotèy, dodin
around   [erawnd] *adv* alantou, otou, anviron
arouse   [erawz] *v* reveye, eksite
arrange   [eranndj] *v* ranje, òganize
array   [arey] *n* etalaj
arrest   [aerèst] *n* arestasyon *v* arete
arrive   [arey] *v* rive
arrogant   [arogaent] *adj* arogan
arrow   [aèro] *n* flèch
art   [art] *n* ar, la
artful   [artfoul] *adj* rize, koken
article   [atik] *n* atik
artificial   [artifichyal] *adj* atifisyèl
as   [az] *adv* tankou, otan, menm ak
ascend   [asennd] *v* monte
ascent   [asent] *v* monte
ascertain   [asèuten] *v* tcheke, rann kont
ashamed   [aechemd] *adj* ront
ashtray   [achtrey] *n* sandriye
aside   [aesayd] *adv* akote, sou kote
ask   [ask] *v* mande
askew   [aeskyou] *adj* krochi
asleep   [aslip] *adj* nan dòmi

aspect   [aspèkt] *n* aspè
asphalt   [asfalt] *n* asfalt
ass   [ass] *n* bourik, dèyè, bounda
assail   [aseyl] *v* asayi, atake
assert   [aesèot] *v* revandike
assign   [aesayn] *v* deziyen, anchaje
assignment   [asaynment] *n* misyon
assist   [asist] *v* ede, segonde
assume   [asyoum] *v* sipoze
assure   [achyour] *v* asire
astonish   [astonich] *v* etone, siprann
astound   [aestawnd] *v* fè sote, pantan
astute   [astyout] *v* rize
asunder   [asondèu] *v* kase ande
asylum   [aesaylòm] *n* azil
athwart   [etfwart] *adv* antravè
atonement   [etonment] *v* redanpsyon
atop   [aetòp] *adv* anlè, soutèt
atrocious   [aetrochyous] *adj* atròs
attach   [aetatch] *v* tache, kole
attack   [aetak] *v* atake
attain   [aeteyn] *v* atenn, rive
attainment   [aetenment] *n* reyalizasyon
attempt   [aetenmpt]*n* esè, tantatif, *v* tante, pran hans
attend   [aetennd] *v* asiste

attention [aetennsyonn] *n* atansyon
attest [aetèst] *v* ateste
attitude [aetityoud] *n* atitud
attract [aetrakt] *v* atire
attribute [aetribyout] *n* kalite
audit [òdit] *v* verifye
August [ògèust] *n* out
aunt [ant] *n* tant, matant
auspicious [ospikuyous] *adj* favorab
austere [ostir] distan, endiferan
author [òtfèu] *n* otè, lotè, ekriven
autumn [otòmn] *n* lotòn
available [aeveylebl] *adj* disponib
avaricious [aevarichyous] *adj* peng, kripya,
   ava
avenge [aevenndj] *v* vanje
avenue [avenyou] *n* avnu
average [avredj] *n* mwayèn
avert [aevèrt] *v* evite, detounen
avid [avid] *adj* avid, grangou
avoid [avoyd] *v* evite
avouch [aevawtch] *v* avalide
awake [aewek] *adj* reveye
award [aewaod] *n* prim
away [aewey] *adv* lwen
awful [òwfoul] *adj* terifyan

163

awhile   [aewayèol] on moman
awkward   [aòkwaòrd] gòch
axe   [aks] *n* rach, aks
axis   [aksis] aks
azure   [azyour] *adj* ble

B

baby [beybi] *n* bebe, timoun
bachelor [batchelèu] *n* selibatè
back [bak] *n* do, reverse
bacon [bekonn] *n* bekonn, la kochon
bad [bad] *adj* move, gate
baffle [bafl] *n* deflektè *v* deroute
bag [bag] *n* sachè
bake [bek] *v* founen
bald [bòld] *adj* chòv
bale [bel] *n* bal *v* anbale
ball [bòl] *n* boul
ball [bòl] *n* boul, balon
ballot [balòt] *n* bilten vòt
ban [benn] *n* entèdiksyon *v* entèdi
band [bend] *n* band, riban, *v* bande
bang [beng] *n* detonasyon, *v* frape
banish [banich] *v* bani
banner [banèu] *n* banyè
banquet [bennkwèt] *n* bivèt, bankè
baptism [baptizm] *n* batèm
bar [bar] *n* bar, kafe
barber [barbèu] *n* kwafè

bare [bèr] *adj* toutouni
bargain [bargen] *n* afè *v* machande
bargaining [bargenin] *n* machandaj
bark [bark] *n* ekòs, po, *v* jape
barley [barli] *n* òj
barren [barenn] *adj* arid, steril
barring [baerin] *prep* sòf, eksepte
barter [bartèu] *n* tròk, *v* troke
base [bes] *n* fondasyon, baz
basement [besment] *n* sousòl
basin [besenn] *n* basen
basket [baskèt] *n* panye
basketball [basket] *n* baskètbòl
bastard [bastaèd] *n* bata
baste [best] *v* aroze
bat [bat] *n* chòvsourit
batch [batch] *n* founen, pake
bath [batf] *n* beny
bathe [betf] *v* benyen
bathrobe [batfrob] *n* dezabiye, moumou
bathroom [batfroum] *n* twalèt
baton [baetonn] *n* baton
batter [batèu] *n* pat pou fri
battery [batèuri] *n* batri
battle [batl] *n* batay
bawl [baol] *n* braye, fè djòlè

bay [bey] *n* rad, gòlf, bè
beach [bitch] *n* plaj
beam [bim] *n* reyon
bean [bin] *n* pwa (rouj)
bear [bèr] *n* lous, ous
beard [bird] *n* bab
beast [bist] *n* bèt (sovaj)
beat [bit] *n* kadans, *v* bat, kale
beautiful [byoutifoul] *adj* bèl
because [bikoz] *conj* paske, akòz
become [bikòm] *v* vini, tounen
bed [bèd] *n* kabann
bedroom [bèdroum] *n* chanm
bee [bi] *n* myèl, abèy
beef [bif] *n* vyann bèf
beer [bir] *n* byè
beet [bit] *n* bètrav
beetle [bitl] *n* skarabe
befall [bifòl] *v* rive
before [bifòr] *prep* avan, anvan
befriend [bifrennd] *v* trete an zanmi
beg [bèg] *v* mande, sipliye
beggar [bègar] *n* mandyan
begin [bigin] *v* kòmanse
beguile [bigwayl] *v* tronpe
behalf [biaf] *n* anfavè

behave [biev] *v* konpòte
behind [bihaynd] *prep* dèyè
behold [bihold] *v* kontanple, gade
being [biying] *n* egzistans, kretyen
belch [bèlch] *v* rote, vomi
belie [bilay] *v* demanti
believe [biliv] *v* kwè
bell [bèl] *n* klòch
bellow [bèlow] begle
belong [bilong] *v* fè pati
below [bilow] *prep* anba
belt [bèlt] *n* senti, sentiron
bench [bennch] *n* ban, bankèt
bend [bend] *v* pliye, koube
beneath [binètf] *prep* anba
beneficence [benefisenns]*n* byenfezans
beneficial [benefichal] *adj* benefisyèl
benefit [benefit] *n* benefis
benevolent [benevolent] *adj* benevòl
berry [beri] *n* grenn
beseech [bisitch] *v* sipliye
beside [bisayd] *prep* akote
besides [bisayds] *prep* dayè
besiege [bisidj] *v* asyeje
best [bèst] *adv* mye, miyò, *adj* meyè, pi bon
bet [bèt] *v* parye

betray [bitrey] *v* trayi
better [bètèu] *adj* pi bon
betting [bèting] *n* parayj
between [bitwin] *prep* ant, nan mitan, omilye
beware [biwèr] *v* mefye
bewilder [bewildèur] *v* dezoryante
bewitch [biwitch] *v* chame, ansòsele
beyond [biyond] *adv* lòtbò
bicycle [baysikl] *n* bisiklèt
bid [bid] *n* òf, pari
bigot [bigòt] *n* fanatik
bile [bayl] *n* kòlè
bilingual [baylingwal] *adj* bileng
bind [baynd] *v* tache, mare, uni
bird [bèurd] *n* zwazo
bitch [bitch] *n* femèl chen
bite [bayt] *v* mòde
bitter [bitèu] *adj* anmè
blab [blab] *v* blabla
black [blak] *adj* nwa
blade [bled] *n* lam
blame [blem] *v* blame, joure
bland [blend] *adj* afab, emab
blank [blenk] *adj* vid, blan
blanket [blengkèt] *n* kouvèti**

blaze   [blez] *n* flanm
bleach   [blitch] *n* kloròks, *v* blanchi
bleak   [blik] *adj* fèb
bleed   [blid] *v* senyen
blessing   [blèsing] *n* benediksyon
blind   [blaynd] *adj* avèg, *n* avèg, je pete
blissful   [blisfoul] *n* byennere
blockhead   [blòkhèd] ennbesil, idyo
blood   [blòd] *n* san
bloom   [bloum] *v* fleri
blossom   [blòsonm] *n* flè
blot   [blòt] *n* tach
blow   [blow] *n* kou, chòk, *v* mouche, soufle, sonnen
blue   [blou] *adj* ble
bluff   [blòf] *n* blòf, *v* blofe
blush   [blòch] *v* rouji, ront
board   [bord] *n* planch, *v* anbake
boast   [bost] *v* vante
boat   [bot] *n* bato, batiman
body   [bòdi] *n* kò
bogus   [bogèus] *adj* fo, atifisyèl
boil   [bòyl] *v* bouyi
bold   [bold] *adj* kare, odasye, temerè
bone   [bon] *n* zo
book   [bouk] *n* liv, *v* arete

boost   [boust] *v* remonte, rechaje
boot   [bout] *n* bòt
border   [bòrdèu] *n* frontyè, bòdi(u), lizyè
bore   [bòr] *v* anniye, *adj* raz
boring   [bòring] *adj* raz, penitan
borrow   [borow] *v* prete
bosom   [bouzonm] *n* tete, pwatrin
boss   [bòs] *n* patron
both   [botf] *adj* toulede
bother   [bòdvèu] *v* anmède, anbete
bottle   [bòtl] *n* boutèy
bottom   [bòtonm] *n* fon, anba, bounda
bough   [bo] *n* branch
bound   [bawnd] *adj* oblije, fòse
boundless   [bawndlès] *adj* san limit
bountiful   [bawntifoul] *adj* abondan, jenere
bouquet   [bouquet] *n* boukè flè, odè
bout   [bawt] *n* atak, peryòd, kriz
bow   [baw] *adj* bankal, *v* koube
bowl   [bowl] *n* bòl
box   [bòks] *n* bwat
boy   [bòy] *n* gason, ti gason
brace   [bres] *v* bretèl, atach
brag   [brag] *v* vante, fè djòlè
brain   [bren] *n* sèvo, tèt
branch   [brennch] *n* branch

brass [bras] *n* kuiv, leton
brave [brev] *adj* brav
brawl [brawl] *n* diskisyon, *v* goumen
brawn [brawn] *n* misk, musk
brawny [brawni] *adj* miskle, muskle
bread [brèd] *n* pen
break [brek] *v* kase, kraze, brize, separe
breakfast [brekfast] *n* kolasyon, dejne
breast [brèst] *n* tete, sen
breath [brètf] *n* alèn, souf
breathe [britf] *v* respire,
breathless [brèflès] *adj* san souf
breed [brid] *v* kwaze, elve
breeze [briz] *n* briz
bribe [brayb] *v* kòronp
brick [brik] *n* brik
bridge [bridj] *n* pon
brief [brif] *adj* brèf, *n* dosye
bright [brayt] *adj* klere, eklere, entelijan, briyan
brilliant [brilyant] *adj* klere, fò
brim [brim] *n* bò, rebò
bring [bring] *v* pote, mennen
brisk [brisk] *adj* chofe, anime
brittle [britl] *adj* frajil, poud
broad [bròd] *adj* laj, liberal

broadcast [bròdkast] *n* emisyon, *v* emèt, voye

broker [brokèu] *n* koutye

brook [brouk] *n* sous, pasdlo, ti rivyè

broom [broum] *n* bale, *v* bale

broth [bròtf] *n* bouyon

brother [bròtvèu] *n* frè

brow [braw] *n* sousi

brown [brawn] *adj* maron

bruise [brouz] *v* mètri

brush [bròch] *n* bròs, *v* brose

brute [brout] *adj* brital, sovaj

bud [bòd] *n* boujon

buffoon [byoufonn] *n* ransè, voryen

bug [bòg] *n* pinèz, ensèk

build [bild] *v* bati, konstwi

bulge [bòldj] *v* gonfle, bonbe

bull [boul] *n* toro

bullet [boulèt] *n* bal

bump [bonp] *n* chòk, kou, *v* frape, pouse

bunch [bonnch] *adj* anpil *n* grap, pakèt

bundle [bonndl] *n* pake, lyas

burglar [bèuglar] *n* vòlè, kanbriyolè

burial [bèuryal] *n* antèman

burn [bèurn] *n* boule *v* boule

burst [bèurst] *v* eklate, pete

bury   [bèuri] *v* antere
bus   [bòs] *n* bis, otobis
bush   [bouch] *n* raje, rak
business   [biznis] *n* afè, negòs
busy   [bizi] *adj* okipe, afere
but   [bòt] *conj* men
butcher   [bòtchèu] *n* bouche
butter   [bèutèu] *n* bè, *v* bere
butterfly   [bèutèuflay] *n* papiyon
button   [bòtonn] *n* bouton
buy   [bay] *v* achte
bypass   [baypas] *n* devyasyon, *v* kontoune
byword   [baywèud] *n* provèb, sinonim

C

cab   [kab] *n* taksi
cabbage   [kabedj] *n* chou
cabin   [kabin] *n* kabin
cable   [kebl]*n* kab, telegram
cache   [kach] *n* kachèt
cachet   [kachèt] *n* grenn, kachè
cadence   [kadenns] *n* kadans
cafe   [kafe] *n* kafe, bwat
cage   [kedj] *n* kalòj
cake   [kek] *n* gato
calamity   [kalamiti] *n* kalamite
calculate   [kalkyulet] *v* kalkile
calf   [kaf] *n* ti bèf
call   [kòl] *v* rele
callous   [kalous] *adj* di, rèd, san pitye
calm   [kalm] *adj* kalm
camel   [kamòl] *n* chamo
camera   [kamra] *n* kamera, kodak
camp   [kenp] *n* kanpman, *v* desann, poze pye
can   [kenn] *n* kanistè, *v* kapab
cancel   [kensèl] *v* anile
cancer   [kennsè] *n* kansè

candid [kenndid] *adj* fran
candle [kenndl] *n* chandèl
candy [kenndi] *n* sirèt, bonbon
cane [ken] *n* kann
canteen [kenntin] *n* kantin
canter [kentèu] *v*trote, *n* ti galope
canvas [kennvas] *n* twal
cap [kap] *n* berè
capable [kepebl] *adj* konpetan
capacity [kapasiti] *n* kapasite
capital [kapitòl] *n* kapital
caption [kapsyonn] *n* antèt, lejand
captious [kaptyous] *adj* acheval, manyak
captivate [kaptivet] *v* kaptive
captive [kaptiv] *adj* kaptif
capture [kaptyèu] *v* kaptire, bare
carcass [karkas] *n* kakas
card [kard] *n* kat, kat jwe
cardigan [kardigann] *n* vès (san manch)
cardinal [kardinal] *n* kadinal
care [care] *n* swen, *v* swanye
careful [kèrfoul] *adj* atantif, apwofondi
caress [kaerès] *n* karès
carpet [karpèt] *n* tapi
carriage [kaeridj] *n* charyo, kabwèt
carrot [kaeròt] *n* karòt

carry   [kaeri] *v* pote

cartoon   [kartoun] *n* komik, desen anime

carve   [karv] *v* sizle, skilte

case   [kes] *n* ka, kès, bwat

cash   [kach] *n* lajan, kach, *adj* kontan

casing   [kesing] *n* anvlòp, amati

cast   [kast] *n* ròl, *v* jete, voye

castigate   [kastiget] *v* reprimande, chatye, joure

castle   [kasl] *n* chato

casual   [kajuòl] *adj* aksidantèl, dezenvòlt

cat   [kat] *n* chat

catch   [katch] *v* pran, bare, *n* lapèch

cater   [katèu] *v* founi, aprovizyone

cathedral   [katfidròl] *n* katedral

cattle   [katl] *n* betay

cause   [kòz] *n* kòz, lakòz, rezon

caution   [kòchonn] *n* prekosyon

cave   [kev] *n* kav, gròt

caviar   [kavyar] *n* kavya, ze

cavity   [kaviti] *n* trou, fant

cease   [siz] *v* sispann, rete, stòp

cede   [sid] *v* sede, bay legen

ceiling   [siling] *n* plafon

celebrate   [selebret] *v* selebre

cellar   [sèla] *n* kav

cemetery   [semetari] *n* simityè
century   [senntyuri] *n* syèk
cereal   [sereyal] *n* sereyal
certain   [sèutenn] *adj* sèten, siswafè
certainly   [sèutennli] *adv* sètènman
certify   [sèutifay] *v* sètifye
chafe   [tchef] *v* frote, friksyonen, irite
chaff   [tchaf] *n* bal, pake pay
chaffer   [tchefèu] *n* anmèdan
chagrin   [cheugrin] *n* kontraryete, chagren
chain   [tchen] *n* chenn
chair   [tchèr] *n* chèz
chairman   [tchèrmann] *n* presidan, direktè
chalk   [tchòk] *n* lakre
chamber   [tchenmbèu] *n* chanm
champ   [tchenp] *n* chanpyon
chance   [tchens] *n* chans
chancel   [tchensèl] *v* titile
chandelier   [tcehndlyèu] chandelye
change   [tchenj] *n* monnen, *v* chanje
chant   [tchent] *n* chante, refren
chap   [tchap] *n* kaskèt, FIG. jenn gason
chapter   [tchaptèu] *n* chapit
characterize   [karakterayz] *v* karakterize
charcoal   [tcharkol] *n* chabon
charge   [tchardj] *n* chaj, *v* chaje

178

charity [tchariti] *n* charite, zèv
charm [tcharm] *n* cham, bèlte
chary [tchari] *v* ezitan, pridan
chase [tches] *v* kouri dèyè, chase
chaste [tchest] *adj* tifi
chat [tchat] *v* koze
cheap [tchip] *adj* bon mache
cheat [tchit] *v* vole, tronpe
check [tchèk] *v* verifye, *n* chèk
checker [tchèkèu] *n* chekè
cheek [tchik] *n* figi, po figi, jou
cheer [tchir] *v* ankouraje, aplodi
cheese [tchiz] *n* fromaj
cherish [tcherich] *v* pran swen
cherry [tcheri] *n* seriz
chess [tchès] *n* echèk
chest [tchèst] *n* pwatrin
chew [tchouw] *v* moulen, mache
chicken [tchikenn] *n* poul
chief [tchif] *n* chèf
child [tchayld] *n* pitit, timoun
chill [tchil] *v* rafredi
chimney [tchimnni] *n* chemine
chin [tchin] *n* manton
china [tchayna] *n* pòslèn
chink [tchink] *v* trenke

choice [tchòys] *n* chwa, preferans
choke [tchok] *n* toufe
choose [tchouz] *v* chwazi
chop [tchòp] *v* tranche, koupe
Christmas [kristmas] *n* Nwèl
chuck [tchòk] *v* flanke deyò
chuckle [tchòkl] *v* ri anbachal
chum [tchonm] *n* zanmi, patnè
chump [tchonp] *v* blòk (bwa)
church [tchèurtch] *n* legliz
cinder [sinndèu] *n* sann
cinema [sinema] *n* sinema
circle [sèurkl] *n* sèk
circular [sèurkyula] *adj* ron, ansèk
circumstance [sèurkonmstenns] *n* sikonstans
circus [sèurkòus] *n* sirk
city [siti] *n* vil, lavil
claim [klem] *n* reklamasyon
clammy [klamy] *adj* mwat
clamp [klanp] *n* kranpon
clang [klenng] *v* sonnen, rezone
clap [klap] *v* aplodi, bat bravo
clarify [klarifay] *v* eklèsi, klarifye
clasp [klasp] *n* agraf
class [klas] *n* klas
clause [klòz] *n* propozisyon

claw   [klòw] *n* grif
clay   [kley] *n* tè glèz, ajil
clean   [klin] *adj* pròp, *v* netwaye
clear   [klir] *adj* klè, transparan, *v* debarase
cleave   [kliv] *v* fann
clement   [klement] *adj* gen pitye
clench   [klennch] *v* mare, sere, ponyen
clergyman [klèudjimann] klèje
clerk   [klèuk] *n* komi
clever   [klivèu] *adj* entelijan
cliff   [klif] *n* falèz
climb   [klaymb] *v* grenpe
cloak   [klok] *n* mask
clock   [klòk] *n* revèy
clod   [klòd] *n* bit tè
close   [kloz] *v* fèmen, *adj* raproche
cloth   [klòtf] *n* twal
clothe   [klotfv] *v* abiye
cloud   [klawd] *n* nuaj, nyaj
clump   [klonp] *n* touf
clumsy   [klonmzi] *adj* gòch, maladwa
cluster   [klòstèu] *n* grap
coal   [kol] *n* chabon
coarse   [kòrs] *adj* koryas
coast   [kost] *n* rivaj, *v* desann sou roulib
coat   [kot] *n* manto, *v* kouvri ak kouch

181

coax [koks] *v* kajole
cobweb [kòbwèb] *n* fil arenyen
cock [kòk] *n* kòk, *v* ame, branche
coddle [kòdl] *v* dòlote
coefficient [koefichent] *n* koefisyan
coerce [kowèus] *v* kontrenn
coffee [kòfi] *n* kafe
coffin [kòfin] *n* sèkèy
cognac [konyak] *n* konyak
cohabit [koabit] *v* koabite
coin [kòyn] *n* (lajan) monnen
coincidence [koinsidenns] *n* konyensidans
cold [kold] *n* fredi, frèt
collaborate [kolaboret] *v* kolabore, soutni
collar [kòlar] *n* kòl, chenn (zannimo)
collect [kòlèkt] *v* rasanble, kolekte
college [kòlèdj] *n* kolèj
colloquial [kolokyòl] *adj* familye
colon [kolonn] *n* kolon, depwen
colonel [kolonèl] *n* kolonèl
color [kòlò] *n* koulè, *v* kolore
column [kòlòmn] *n* kolòn, pilye
comb [konb] *n* peny
come [kòm] *v* vini
comfort [konmfòt] *n* konfò, *v* rekonfòte
comfortable [konmfòtebl] *adj* konfòtab

command [kòmennd] *n* kòmann, *v* kòmande
commence [komenns] *v* kòmanse
commend [kòmennd] *n* lòd, *v* kòmande, òdone
commerce [kòmèus] *n* komès, negòs
commit [kòmit] *v* komèt,
common [kòmonn] *adj* komen
communicate [komyouniket] *v*kominike
compare [konmpèu] *v* konpare
competition [konmpetichonn] *n* konkou, konpetisyon
complain [konmplen] *v* plenyen
complete [konmplit] *v* konplete, *adj* konplè
compose [konmpoz] *v* konpoze
compound [konmpawnd] *n* konpoze, alyaj
comprehend [konmprehend] *v* konprann
comrade [konmrad] *n* kanmarad
conceal [konnsil] *v* kache
concept [konnsèpt] *n* konsèp
concise [konnsayz] *adj* brèf, kout
conclude [konnkloud] *v* konkli
concrete [konnkrit] *n* siman, *adj* konkrè
condemn [konndèm] *v* kondane
condition [konndichonn] *n* kondisyon
condone [konndon] *v* favorize
conduct [konndòkt] *v* kondui, *n* konduit

confectionery [konnfekchonèri] *n* sirèt
confess [konnfès] *v* konfese
confident [konnfident] *adj* asire, gen
  konfyans
confirm [konnfèum] *v* konfime
conform [konnfòm] *v* konfòme, *adj* konfòm
confuse [konfyouz] *adj* egare, gaga
confusion [konfyoujonn] *n* konfizyon
congest [konndjèst] *v* bloke, konjeste,
  bouche
congratulate [konngratyoulet] *v* fè
  konpliman
congregate [konngreget] *v* reyini, rasanble
conjecture [konndjektchèu] *n* konjekti
conjoin [konndjòyn] *n* konjwen
connect [konèkt] *v* konekte
connive [konayv] *v* fè payas
conquer [konnkèu] *v* konkeri
conscience [konnchyenns] *n* konsyans
conscious [konnchyous] *adj* gen konesans
consent [konnsent] *v* konsanti
consequence [konnskwenns] *n* konsekans
consider [konnsidèu] *v* konsidere
consist [konnsist] *v* konsiste
console [konnsol] *v* konsole
consolidate [konnsolidet] *v* konsolide

constant [konnstent] *n* konstant, *adj*
  konstan, èmanan
constitute [konntityout] *v* konstitye
constrain [konnstren] *v* rennen, frennen,
  kontrenn
construct [konnstròkt] *v* konstrui
consult [konnsòlt] *v* konsilte, mande konsèy
contaminate [konntaminet] *v* kontamine
contempt [konntenmpt] *n* mepri
contend [konntennd] *v* deklare, soutni,
  kenbe
content [konntent] *adj* satisfè, *n* kontni
contest [konntèst] *n* konpetisyon, konkou
continue [konntinyou] *v* kontinye
contort [konntòrt] *v* kontòsyone
contract [konntrakt] *n* kontra
contradict [konntradikt] *v* kontredi
contrary [konntrari] *adj* kontrè, opoze
contravene [konntraèvin] *v* kontredi,
  kontrekare
contribute [konntribyout] *v* kontribye
convene [konnvin] *v* konvoke, reyini
convenient [konnvinyent] *adj* pratik
convention [konnvennchonn] *n* konvansyon
conversation [konnvèusechonn] *n*
  konvèsasyon, koze

185

convey   [konnvey] *v* transmèt

convict   [konnvikt] *n* kondane, *v* deklare
  koupab

convince   [konnvins] *v* konvenk

cook   [khouk] *n* m. kizinye, f. kizinyè

cool   [khoul] *adj* frèt

cop   [khòp] *n* jandam

cope   [khop] *v* debouye, abitye

copper   [khòpèu] *n* kuiv

copy   [khòpi] *v* kopye, *n* kopi

cord   [khòrd] *n* kòd

cork   [khòrk] *n* bouchon lyèj

corn   [khòrn] *n* mayi

corner   [khòrnèu] *n* kwen, *v* kwense, bare

cornflower   [khòrnflawèu] *n* flè mayi

corpse   [khòrps] *n* kadav

correct   [khorèkt] *adj* kòrèk, *v* korije

correspond   [khòresponnd] *v* koresponn, ekri

corrode   [korod] *v* rouye

corrup   [koròpt] *v* kòronp

cost   [kòst] *v* koute, *n* pri

cotton   [kòtonn] *n* koton

couch   [kawtch] *n* kanape

cough   [kòf] *n* tous, *v* touse

council   [kawnsil] *n* konsèy

count   [kawnt] *n* dekont, *v* konte

186

country [kawntri] *n* peyi
county [kawnti] *n* depatman
couple [kòpl] *n* koup, pè, *v* marye, kole
courage [kèuredj] *n* kouraj
course [kohèus] *n* kous
court [koèurt] *n* tribinal, lakou
courteous [koèutous] *adj* koutwa
cousin [koèuzenn] *n* m. kouzen, f. kouzin
covenant [kovenent] *n* akò, konvansyon
cover [kòvèu] *n* kouvèti, proteksyon, *v* kouvri
cow [kaw] *n* bèf, vach
coward [kawèud] *n* kapon
crack [khrak] *n* krak, fant
cradle [kredl] *n* bèso
crafty [krafti] *adj* rize, abil
cram [krenm] *v* boure, bachote
crash [khrach] *n* fraka, *v* kraze
crave [krev] *v* anvi
crawl [krawl] *v* ranpe
crayfish [khrefich] *n* kribich
crazy [khrezi] *adj* fou
creak [khrik] *v* krake
cream [khrim] *n* krèm
create [khriyet] *v* kreye
creature [khritchèu] *n* kreyati, kretyen

credit [khredit] *n* kredi, *v* kredite
creed [khrid] *n* kredo
creek [khrik] *n* rivyè
creep [khrip] *v* ranpe, glise
Creole [kriol] *adj* kreyòl
crew [khrou] *n* ekip
crib [khrib] *n* bèso
crime [khraym] *n* krim
cripple [khripl] *v* estropye, *n* enfim
crisp [krisp] *adj* sèk
crook [krouk] *n* vòlè
crop [kròp] *n* rekòlt
cross [kròs] *n* kwa, *v* travèse, kwaze
crow [kro] *n* kònèy
crowd [krawd] *n* foul, *v* ankonbre
crucify [krusifay] *v* krisifye
crude [krud] *adj* kri, grosye
cruel [kroul] *adj* kriyèl, mechan
cruise [krouz] *n* kwazyè
crumb [kronmb] *n* krout, myèt
crush [kròch] *v* kraze
crust [kròst] *n* krout
cry [khray] *v* kriye
cucumber [kyoukonmbèu] *n* konkonm
cult [kòlt] *n* kilt
culture [kèultchèu] *n* kilti, koutcha

cunning   [konning] *adj* malen
cup   [kòp] *n* gode
curd   [kèurd] *n* lètkaye
cure   [kyour] *v* swanye, *n* remèd, tretman
curious   [kuryous] *adj* kirye
curl   [kèurl] *n* pli
currency   [kèurennsi] *n* lajan
current   [kèurent]*adj* kouran *n* kouran
  elektrik
curse   [kèurs] *n* malediksyon, *v* joure, modi
curtain   [kèurten] *n* rido
cushion   [kouchonn] *n* kousen
custody   [kèustodi] *n* siveyans
custom   [kèustonm] *n* ladwan, koutim
cut   [kòt] *v* koupe
cute   [kyout] *adj* bèl
cycle   [saykl] *n* bisiklèt

D

dabble   [dabl] *v* babote
daddy   [dadi] *n* papa
daft   [daft] *adj* idyo, bèt
daily   [deli] *adj* toulejou
dally   [dali] *v* lanbinen
dam   [denm] *n* baraj
damage   [damedj] *n* domaj, *v* domaje
damn   [damn denm] *v* modi
damp   [denp] *adj* mouye, mwat
dance   [denns] *n* dans, *v* danse
danger   [denndjèu] *n* danje
dare   [dèr] *v* defye, bay gabèl
dark   [dark] *adj* fonse, nwa
darling   [darling] *adj* cheri
darn   [darn] *v* reprize
dart   [dart] *n* flèch, javlo, *v* plonje
dash   [dach] *v* detale, *n* priz
data   [deta] *n* done, eleman
daughter   [dòtèu] *n* pitit fi, tifi
daunt   [dont] *v* dekouraje, entimide
dawdle   [dawdl] *v* lanbinen, ranse
dawn   [dòrn] *n* devanjou, avanjou

day [dey] *n* jou, jounen

dazzle [dazl] *v* eblouyi, avegle (pete) je

dead [dèd] *adj* mouri, mò

deaden [dèdenn] amòti, mouri

deadlock [dèdlòk] *adj* enpas

deaf [dèf] *adj* soud

deal [dhil] *v* distribye, bay

dear [dhir] *adj* chè, cheri

dearth [dèurf] *n* grangou, famin

death [dèf] *n* lanmò

debase [dhibes] *v* abese, avili

debate [dhibet] *v* debat, diskite

debauch [debotch] *n* debòch

debt [dèt] *n* dèt

decay [dhikey] *v* pouri, dekonpoze

deceive [dhisiv] *v* desevwa, bay koutba

December [dhisenmbèu] *n* desanm

deception [dhisèpchonn] *n* desepsyon

decide [dhisayd] *v* deside

decision [desijyonn] *n* desizyon

deck [dèk] *n* platfòm, pon

declare [dhiklèr] *v* deklare

decline [dhiklayn] *v* refize, bese

decorate [dekoret] *v* dekore

decoy [dhikòy] *n* payas

decrease [dhikriz] *v* diminye

decree [dhikri] *n* dekrè
deed [dhid] *n* aksyon
deep [dhip] *adj* fon
default [dhifòlt] *n* defo
defeat [dhifit] *v* bat, venk
defect [dhifèkt] *n* defo fabrik
defense [dhifenns] *n* defans
defer [dhifèu] *v* ranvwaye
definite [definit] definitif
deft [dèft] *adj* ajil
defy [dhifay] *v* defye, pini
degree [dhigrih] *n* degre, grad, diplòm
delay [dhiley] *v* retade
delete [dhilit] *v* efase
deliberate [deliberet] *adj* esprè
deliberate [deliberet] *v* reflechi, debat
delicate [deliket] *adj* delika
delicious [delisyous] *adj* bon gou
delight [delayt] *n* plezi
delirious [diliryous] *adj* delala, fou
deliver [delivèu] *v* delivre
deluge [delyouj] *n* delij, inondasyon
delve [delve] *v* fouye
demand [demand] *n* demann, *v* mande
demolish [dimòlich] *v* demoli
dense [denns] *adj* epè

192

deny [dinay] *v* renye
department [dipartment] *n* depatman
departure [dipartyèu] *n* depa
depend [dipennd] *v* depann
depict [depikt] *v* dekri, demontre
deport [dipòrt] *v* depòte
depose [dipoz] *v* dechouke
deposit [depozit] *n* depo, *v* depoze
depot [dipo] *n* depo
deprave [diprev] *v* detounen
depress [diprès] *v* peze
depth [dèf] *n* pwofondè
descend [disennd] *v* desann
describe [diskrayb] *v* dekri
desert [dèzèut] *n* dezè
deserve [dizèuv] *v* merite
design [dizayn] *n* desen, *v* desine
desire [dizayèu] *v* anvi, vle
desk [dèsk] *n* biwo
despair [dispèr] *v* dezespere
desperate [dèspret] *adj* dezespere, atoufè
despite [dispayt] *adv* malgre
dessert [dizèut] *n* desè
destiny [dèstini] *n* destine
destroy [distròy] *v* detwi, kraze
detach [ditatch] *v* detache

detail   [diteyl] *n* detay

detain   [diteyn] *v* kenbe, arete

detect   [ditèkt] *v* detekte

deter   [ditèu] *v* anpeche

determined   [ditèumind] *adj* detèmine, antete

detest   [ditèst] *v* deteste, rayi

detour   [ditor] *n* detou

devastate   [devastet] *v* devaste

develop   [divèlòp] *v* devlope

device   [divays] *n* enstriman

devil   [dèvil] *n* demon

devout   [divaout] *adj* devwe

dew   [dou] *n* larouze

diary   [dayari] *n* jounal pèsonèl

dictionary   [diksyonèri] *n* diksyonè

die   [day] *v* mouri

differ   [difèu] *v* pa dakò

different   [difrent] *adj* diferan

difficult   [difikòlt] *adj* difisil

dig   [dig] *v* fouye

digest   [daydjèst] *n* ekstrè, *v* dijere

dignity   [digniti] *n* diyite

diligent   [dilidjent] *adj* debouya

dilute   [daylyout] *v* delye

dim   [dim] *adj* pal

dinner [dinèu] *n* dine
dip [dip] *v* plonje
direct [dirèkt] *adj* dirèk, *v* dirije
dirt [dèut] *n* kras, pousyè, salte
dirty [dèuti] *adj* sal
disable [disebl] *v* deranje
disabled [disebl] *adj* andikape, enfim
disagree [disagri] *v* pa dakò
disagreeable [disagriyabl] *adj* dezagreyab
disappear [disapir] *v* disparèt
disappoint [disapoynt] *v* desevwa
disapprove [desaprouv] *v* dezaprouve
disarray [diserey] *n* tètchaje
disaster [dizastèu] *n* dezas
disburse [disbèus] *v* debouse
discern [disèun] *v* dekouvri, disène
discharge [distcharj] *v* vide
discontent [diskonntent] *n* mekontantman
discord [diskòd] *n* dezakò
discover [diskòvèu] *v* dekouvri
discrete [diskrit] *adj* diskrè
discretion [diskrechonn] *n* diskresyon
discuss [diskòs] *v* diskite
disdain [disden] *n* deden
disease [diziz] *n* maladi
disgrace [disgres] *n* dezonè, wont

195

disgust [disgòst] *n* degou
dish [dich] *n* asyèt, plat
dismiss [dismis] *v* lage, ranvwaye
disorder [dizòrdèu] *n* dezòd
disown [dison] *v* deposede
dispensary [dispennseri] *n* dispansè
display [displey] *v* etale, etale
dissipate [disipet] *v* gaye
distance [distans] *n* distans
distinct [distenkt] *adj* disten, klè
distinguish [distingwich] *v* distenge
distort [distòrt] *v* defòme
distract [distrakt] *v* distrè
distribute [distribyout] *v* distribye
district [distrikt] *n* distri
disturb [distèub] *v* deranje
ditch [ditch] *n* ravin, twou
dive [dayv] *v* plonje
diver [dayvèu] *n* dayiva
diverse [divèus] *adj* divès
divide [divayd] *v* divize
divorce [divòrs] *n* divòs
dizzy [dizi] *adj* gen vètij
do [dou] *v* fè, fabrike
dog [dòg] *n* chen
doll [dòl] *n* poupe

dollar [dòla] *n* dola
domestic [domèstik] *adj* peyi, *n* restavèk
donkey [donnki] *n* bourik
doom [doum] *n* fayit
door [dòr] *n* pòt
dormitory [dòrmitori] *n* dòtwa
dot [dòt] *n* pwen, tach
double [dòbl] *adj* doub, *v* double
doubt [dawt] *n* dout, *v* doute
dough [do] *n* pat farin
dove [dov] *n* pijon
down [dawn] *adv* anba, *v* desann
draft [draft] *n* kourandè, *v* anrole
drag [drag] *v* trennen
drain [dren] *n* egou
draw [drò] *v* rale
drawback [dròbak] *n* dezavantaj
dream [drim] *n* rèv
dreary [driri] *adj* tris, sonm
dress [drès] *n* ròb, *v* abiye
drift [drift] *v* flote
drill [dril] *n* dril, *v* fè egzèsis
drink [drink] *n* bweson, *v* bwè
drip [drip] *v* degoute
drive [drayv] *v* kondui
driver [drayvèu] *n* chofè, kondiktè

drizzle　[drizl] *v* farinen
drop　[dròp] *n* gout *v* lage
drought　[drawt] *n* sechrès
drown　[drawn] *v* nwaye
drug　[dròg] *n* dròg
drum　[dronm] *n* droum
drunk　[dronk] *adj* sou
dry　[dray] *adj* sèk
duck　[dòk] *n* kanna
dull　[dòl] *adj* mat
dumb　[donm] *adj* enbesil, gaga
dump　[donp] *n* pil fatra, *v* jete
dune　[dun] *n* pilsab
dung　[dong] *n* fimye
during　[dyouring] pandan
dusk　[dòsk] labrin
dust　[dòst] pousyè
duty　[dyouti] dwa, taks
dwarf　[dwòrf] tinen
dwelling　[dwèling] *n* kay
dye　[day] *v* kolore

E

each [itch] *adj* chak

eager [igèu] *adj* enterese

eagle [igèul] *n* èg, malfini

ear [ir] *n* zòrèy

early [èurli] *adv* bonè, annavans

earn [èurn] *v* genyen, posede, fè lajan

earnest [èurnèst] *n* bònfwa

earring [iring] *n* zanno

earth [èurf] *n* latè, tè

east [ist] *n* lès

Easter [istèu] *n* Pak

easy [izi] *adj* fasil

eat [it] *n* manje

echo [eko] *n* eko

edge [èdj] *n* kwen, bout

edit [edit] *v* edite

editor [editèu] *n* editè

educate [edyuket] *v* edike

eel [ihl] *n* zangi

efface [ifehs] *v* efase

effort [èfòt] *n* efò, jefò, fòs

egg [èg] *n* ze

eight [eyht] *adj* uit

eighteen [eyhtin] *adj* dizuit

eighty [eyhti] *adj* katreven

either [idvèu] *adj* nenpòt, oswa

eject [idjèkt] *v* retire, pouse soti

elaborate [ilaboreht] *adj* konplike, *v* elabore

elbow [èlbo] *n* koud

elder [eldèu] *n* granmoun

elect [elèkt] *v* chwazi, eli

elephant [elefant] *n* elefan

eleven [ilèvenn] *adj* onz

eliminate [eliminet] *v* elimine

else [èls] *conj* osinon

embassy [enmbasi] *n* anbasad

embellish [enmbelich] *v* anbeli

embolden [enmboldenn] *v* bay kouraj

embrace [enmbres] *v* anbrase, kwoke

embroider [enmbroydèu] *v* brode

emit [emit] *v* emèt, fè sikile

emotion [imochonn] *n* emosyon

employ [enmplòy] *n* djòb, *v* anplwaye

empower [enmpawèu] *v* otorize

empty [enmpti] *adj* vid, *v* vide

enclose [enkloz] *v* fèmen, bouche

encourage [ennkèuredj] *v* ankouraje

encroach [ennkwotch] *v* pyete

end   [ennd] *n* fen, bout

endurance   [enndyurenns] *n* andirans

enemy   [ènmi] *n* lenmi

engage   [enngedj] *v* angaje, foure

engine   [enndjin] *n* motè, machin

English   [inglich] *adj* angle

enigma   [enigma] *n* enigm, magouy

enjoy   [enndjòy] *v* jwi, rejwi, benefisye

enormous   [enòrmous] *adj* enòm, manman, papa

enough   [inòf] *adj* ase, *adv* ase, kont

enrage   [ennredj] *v* enève, agase

enrich   [ennritch] *v* anrichi

enroll   [ennrol] *v* anrole, rekrite

ensure   [ennchèu] *v* asire

entangle   [enntengèul] *v* melanje, mele

enter   [enntèu] *v* antre

enterprise   [enntèuprayz] *n* antrepriz

entertain   [enntèutehn] *v* amize

entice   [entays] *v* enstige, fè lasisiy

entire   [enntayèu] *adj* antye, tout

entrails   [enntrelz] *n* zantray

entrance   [enntranns] *n* antre, pòt

envelope   [ennvlop] *n* anvlòp, *v* vlope

envious   [ennvyous] *adj* anvye

envy   [annvi] *n* anvi

equal [ikwòl] *adj* egal, *v* egale
equip [ekwip] *v* ekipe
equipment [ekwipment] *n* ekipman
erase [irehs] *v* efase
erect [erèkt] *adj* dwat, vètikal, *n* drese, monte
errand [èrannd] *n* komisyon
error [èrèu] *n* erè, fòt
erupt [eròpt] *v* eklate, pete
eruption [eròpsyonn] *n* eklatman
escape [eskep] *v* sove, chape
escort [èskòt] *n* konpayon, *v* eskòte
especial [espechòl] *adj* espesyal
especially [espechèuli] *adv* espesaylman
espionage [espyonaj] *n* espyonaj
esquire [eskwayèu] *n* avoka
establish [establich] *v* etabli
esteem [estim] *n* estim
estimate [estimeht] *n* evalyasyon, *v* estime, valye
evade [ivehd] *v* evade, sove
evangel [evannjèl] *n* levanjil
evangelize [evannjelayz] *v* preche
even [ivenn] *adj* egal, jis, *adv* menm
evening [ivning] *n* aswè, sware
event [ivent] *n* evenman

every [ehvri] *adj* chak
evict [evikt] *v* chase
evident [evident] *adj* evidan, aklè
evil [ivèul] *adj* move
exact [egzakt] *adj* egzak
exaggerate [egzadjereht] *v* egzajere
example [egzenpèul] *n* egzanp
exceed [eksihd] *v* depase, eksede
except [eksèpt] *prp* eksepte
exception [eksèpchonn] *n* eksepsyon
exchange [ekstchannj] *n* twòk, echanj
excite [eksayt] *v* eksite
exclud [eksklud] *v* eskli, retire
excuse [ekskyouz] *n* eskiz, *v* eskize
execute [egzekyout] *v* egzekite, akonpli
exemplary [egzenmpla] *adj* egzanplè
exempt [egzenpt] *adj* egzan
exercise [egsèusayz] *n* egzèsis
exert [egzèurt] *v* fè egzèsis, fose
exhale [ekshel] *v* rann souf, egzale
exhaust [egzost] *n* mòflè, *v*
exist [egzist] *v* egziste
expect [ekspèkt] *v* tann, alatant
expecting [ekspèkting] *n* ansent, gwòs
expel [ekspèl] *v* ranvwaye
expend [ekspennd] *v* elaji, etann

expense [ekspenns] *n* depans
expensive [ekspennsiv] *adj* chè
experience [ekspiryanns] *n* eksperyans
expert [ekspèurt] *n* ekspè
explain [eksplen] *v* eksplike
explicit [eksplisit] *adj* eksplisit, klè
explode [eksplod] *v* eksploze, eklate
explore [eksplòr] *v* eksplore, chèche
explosion [eksplojonn] *n* eksplozyon,
    eklatman
export [ekspòrt] *n* ekspòtasyon, *v* ekspòte
expose [ekspoz] *v* ekspoze
exposition [ekspozichonn] *n* ekspozisyon
express [eksprès] *v* eksprime
extend [ekstennd] *v* etann, ouvri
extent [ckstcnt] *n* limit
exterior [eksteryèu] *n* deyò, eksteryè
external [ekstèunal] *adj* andeyò
extort [ekstòrt] *v* peze
extract [ekstrakt] *n* ekstrè, esans, *v* rale
extraordinary [ekstraòrdinèri] *adj*
    ekstraòdinè
extreme [ekstrim] *adj* ekstrèm
extricate [ekstriket] *v* rache
eye [ay] *n* je, zye
eyebrow [aybraw] *n* sousi

204

F

fable   [febl] *n* istwa, fab
face   [fes] *n* figi, *v* gade (anfas), afwonte
facile   [fasil] *adj* fasil
fact   [fakt] *n* verite
fad   [fad] *n* kapris
fade   [fed] *adj* fennen, *v* disparèt
fail   [feyl] *v* rate
faint   [fent] *adj* pal
fair   [fèr] *adj* jis, ekitab
faith   [fetf] *n* lafwa
fake   [fek] *adj* krizokal, djanni, *v* kapwonnen
fall   [fòhl] *v* tonbe
false   [fòls] *adj* fo, pa vre, manti
family   [famili] *n* fanmi
famine   [famin] *n* famin, grangou
famous   [femous] *adj* enpòtan, gran
fan   [fan] *n* vantilatè, *v* soufle
fancy   [fennsi] *adj* anpenpan *v* imajine
fang   [fenng] *n* kwòk, dan
far   [fahr] *adv* lwen
farm   [fahm] *n* plantasyon, jaden
farther   [fahrdvèu] *adv* pilwen

fascinate   [fasinet] *v* fasine, entrige
fashion   [fachonn] *n* lamòd
fast   [fast] *adj* vit, rapid
fasten   [fasenn] *v* tache, mare
fat   [fat] *adj* gra, epè
fate   [fet] *n* sò, destine
father   [fahdvèu] *n* papa
fatigue   [faetig] *n* fatig
fault   [fòlt] *n* fòt, *v* bay tò
favor   [fevèu] *n* favè, *v* prefere
fear   [fihr] *n* lapè, *v* pè
feast   [fist] *n* bambòch, babako
feather   [fèdvèu] *n* plim
feature   [fityèu] *n* karakteristik, mak
February   [februèri] *n* fevriye
fee   [fi] *n* dwa {ladwann}, frè {depans}
feeble   [fibl] *adj* fèb
feed   [fihd] *v* nouri, bay manje
feel   [fihl] *v* santi
feign   [feyn] *v* fente, pran pòz
felon   [fèlonn] *n* kriminel
female   [fimel] *adj* femèl, *n* fanm
fence   [fenns] *n* baryè, lantouray
fern   [fèurn] foujè
ferocious   [ferochyous] *adj* feròs
fertile   [fèutayl] *adj* donnen, fètil

fetch [fètch] *v* chèche
fever [fivèu] *n* lafyèv
few [fyou] *adj* kèk
fib [fib] *n* manti *v* bay (fè) manti
fiction [fikchonn] *n* fiksyon
fiddle [fidl] *v* jwe ak
field [fild] *n* teren, jaden
fierce [firs] *adj* feròs, terib
fifteen [fiftihn] *adj* kenz
fifty [fifti] *adj* senkant
fight [fayt] *n/v* goumen, batay
file [fayl] *n* dosye, dokiman
fill [fihl] *v* plen
filthy [fihltfi] *adj* sal
final [faynal] *adj* final
find [faynd] *v* jwenn
fine [fayn] *adj* anfòm, fen, *n* amann
finger [fingèu] *n* dwèt, *v* tate, tripote
finish [finich] *v* fini
fire [fayè] *n* dife, *v* revoke
firm [fèurm] *adj* solid, *n* entrepriz
first [fèurst] *adj* premye
fish [fich] *n* pwason
fist [fist] *n* pwen
five [fayv] *adj* senk
fix [fiks] *v* ranje

flag [flag] *n* drapo
flame   [flem] *n* flanm
flash   [flash] *v* klere
flat   [flat] *adj* plat
flavor   [flevèu] *n* gou
flea   [fli] *n* pis, pinèz
flesh   [flèch] *n* vyann, chè
flight   [flayt] *n* vòl {avyon}
flimsy   [flimzi] *adj*
flinch   [flinch] *v* flechi, tresayi
fling   [fling] *v* voye jete
flint   [flint] *n* silèks
flip   [flip] *v* baskile
flirt   [flèurt] *v* file
float   [flot] *v* flote
flock   [flòk] *n* troup, bann
flood   [flòd] *n* inondasyon, *v* anvayi
flour   [flawèu] *n* farin
flow   [flo] *v* koule
flower   [flawèu] *n* flè, *v* fleri
flu   [flou] *n* grip
fluent   [flouent] *adj* kouran
fluid   [flouid] *n* likid
flush   [flòch] *adj* kole, *v* chase, vide
fly   [flay] *n* mouch, *v* vole
foe   [foe] *n* lenmi

fog [fòg] *n* bouya
fold [fold] *n* pli, *v* pliye
folk [fok] *adj* peyi
follow [fòlow] *v* suiv
fond [fonnd] *adj* fanatik
food [foud] *n* manje
fool [foul] *n* enbesil, *v* twonpe
foot [fout] *n* pye
for [fòr] *prp* pou, paske
forbid [fòbid] *v* defann, pini
force [fòrs] *n* fòs, *v* fòse
forecast [fòrkast] *v* projte
foreign [fòrèn] *adj* etranje
foreman [fòmann] *n* bòs, fòmann
forest [fòrèst] *n* forè, rakbwa
forever [fòrèvèu] *adv* ajamè
forget [fògèt] *v* bliye
forgive [fògiv] *v* padonnen
fork [fòrk] *n* fouchèt, *n* ranmase
form [fòrm] *n* fòm, *v* fòme
former [fòmèu] *adj* ansyen
forsake [fòsek] *v* lage, abandone
fortune [fòtyoun] *n* richès, fòtin
forty [fòrti] *adj* karant
forward [fòwòd] *adj* devan, *v* avanse
four [fòhr] *adj* kat

fowl [fawl] *n* volay
fracture [fraktyèu] *n* frakti
fragile [fragayl] *adj* frajil
frame [frem] *n* ankadreman
frank [frenk] *adj* fran
fraud [fròd] *n* fròd
frazzle [frazl] *adj* {kò} kraze, erente
freak [frik] *n* sanzatann
free [fri] *adj* lib, gratis
freedom [fridonm] *n* libète
freeze [frihz] *v* glase, konjle
frequent [frikwent] *adj* souvan
fresh [frèch] *adj* fre, {frekan}
Friday [frayde] *n* vandredi
friend [frenn] *n* zanmi
fright [frayt] *n* freyè, laperèz
frog [fròg] *n* krapo
front [front] *n/prp* devan
frost [fròst] *n* glas
frown [frawn] *v* gwonde, mare min
fruit [frout] *n* fwi
frustration [freustrechonn] *n* fristrasyon
fry [fray] *v* fri
fuel [fyoul] *n* gaz
fulfill [foulfil] *v* ranpli, akonpli
full [foul] *adj* plen

fume   [fume] *n* vapè
fun   [fonn] *adj* amizan, *n* amizman
funeral   [fyouneral] *n* lantèman, fineray
funny   [fonni] *adj* komik
furious   [fyouryous] *adj* firye
furniture   [fèurnityèu] *n* mèb
further   [fèurdvèu] *adv* pilwen
fuss   [fòs] *n* gagòt, meli melo
future   [fyoutyèu] *n* avni

G

gain [gen] *n* benefis, gen, *v* akeri
gall [gal] *n* fyèl, bil
gallon [galonn] *n* galon
game [gem] *n* jwèt
gang [genng] *n* klik
gap [gap] *n* fant
garage [geuradj] *n* garaj
garden [gardenn] *n* jaden flè, patè
gardener [gardenèu] *n* jadinye
garlic [garlik] *n* lay
garment [garment] *n* abiyman, rad
gas [gas] *n* gaz
gate [get] *n* pòtay
gather [gadvèu] *v* ranmase
gauge [gedj] *n* gedj, *v* tcheke
gaze [gez] *v* fikse, kontanple
general [djenròl] *adj/n* jeneral
generate [djèneret] *v* jenere, pwodui
generous [djenerous] *adj* jenere
genesis [djenesis] *n* jenèz
gentle [djenntl] *adj* janti, soupl
get [gèt] *v* pran

ghost [gost] *n* fantom, zonbi

giant [djayant] *adj* jeyan

gift [gift] *n* kado, don

giggle [gigl] *v* griyen

gin [gin] *n* djin

girl [gèurl] *n* tifi, djal

give [giv] *v* bay

give up [givòp] *v* lage, abandone

glad [glad] *adj* kontan

glance [gelnns] *v* gade

glare [glèr] *n* ekla

glass [glas] *n* vit, vè

gleam [glim] *v* miwate

glide [galyd] *v* glise

glitter [glitèu] *n* ekla

globe [glob] glòb

gloom [gloum] *n* tenèb

glory [glori] *n* laglwa

glove [glov] *n* gan

glue [glou] *n* lakòl

gnat [nat] *n* papiyon lanp

go [go] *v* ale

goal [gol] *n* objektif

goat [got] *n* kabrit

god [gòd] *n* espri, lwa

God [gòd] *n* Bondye

gold   [gold] *n* lò
golden   [goldenn] *adj* annò
good   [goud] *adj* bon
goods   [gouds] *n* danre
goose   [gous] *n* zwa
gossip   [gòsip] tripotay
govern   [gòvèun] *v* gouvène
gown   [gawn] *n* ròb
grab   [grab] *v* dapiyan, pran pa fòs
grace   [gres] *n* lagras
grade   [gred] *n* grad, *v* evalye, nivle
graduate   [gradyuet] *n* diplome
grain   [grenn] *n* grenn
grandchild   [granntchayld] *n* ptiti-pitit
grandfather   [grannfadvèu] *n* gran-papa
grandmother   [grannmòdvèu] *n* grann
grape   [grep] *n* rezen
grasp   [grasp] *v* atrap
grass   [gras] *n* zèb
grate   [gret] *v* graje
gratitude   [gratityoud] *n* rekonesans
grave   [grev] *adj* grav, *n* tonm
gravel   [gravèl] *n* gravye
gravy   [grevi] *n* sòs
gray   [gre] *adj* gri
grease   [gris] *n* grès, *v* grese

great [gret] *adj* gran, gwo
greedy [grihdi] *adj* vòlè, visye
green [grihn] *adj* vèt, vè
greet [griht] *v* salye
grief [grihf] *n* chagren, lapenn
grime [graym] *n* salte
grin [grin] *v* ri jòn
grind [graynd] *v* moulen
grinder [grayndèu] *n* moulen
grip [grip] *n* priz
grocery [gròsri] *n* pwovizyon
ground [grawnd] *n* teren, tè
group [gwoup] *n* gwoup, *v* gwoupe
grow [gro] *v* grandi
guard [gard] *n* gad, jandam, *v* gade, siveye
guess [gès] *v* devine
guest [gèst] *n* envite
guide [gayd] *n* gid, *v* gide
guilty [gilti] *adj* koupab
gulp [gòlp] *n* gòje, *v* vale
gum [gonm] *n* gonm, chiklèt, *v* gonmen
gun [gonn] *n* revolvè, kanno
gust [gòst] *n* rafal
gut [gòt] *n* zantray
guy [gay] *n* nèg
Gypsy [djipsi] *n* djipsi

215

H

habit   [habit] *n* abitid
hack   [hak] *v* chire, rache
haggle   [hagl] *v* machande
hair   [hèr] *n* cheve, pwal
half   [haf] *adj* demi, *n* mwatye
hall   [hòl] *n* koridò, òl
ham   [ham] *n* janbon
hammer   [hamèu] *n* mato
hand   [hennd] *n* men
handcuffs   [henndkòfs] *n* menòt
handkerchief   [henkèutchif] *n* mouchwa
handle   [henndl] *n* manch, *v* manyen,
   touche, okipe
handsome   [hennsonm] bèl
handy   [henndi] *adj* itil, *adv* sou la men
hang   [henng] *v* pann, kwoke
happen   [happen] *v* rive, pase
happy   [hapi] *adj* kontan
harbor   [harbòr] *n* pò, waf
hard   [hard] *adj* di
harm   [harm] *v* maltrete
harvest   [harvèst] *v* rekòlte

haste   [hest] *n* anpresman
hat   [hat] *n* chapo
hate   [het] *n* èn, rayisman, *v* rayi
haul   [hòl] *v* bwote, chaje
have   [hav] *v* genyen
haven   [hevenn] *n* azil
hawk   [hawk] *n* malfini
hay   [hey] *n* zèb
he   [hi] *prn* li
head   [hèd] *n* tèt, *v* dirije
headache   [hèdèk] *n* maltèt
health   [hèlf] *n* sante, lasante
healthy   [hèlfi] *adj* ansante
heap   [hihp] *n* pil
heart   [hart] *n* kè, mitan
heaven   [hèvenn] *n* syèl, paradi
heavy   [hèvi] *adj* lou, peze
hedge   [hèdj] *n* bòdi, lizyè
heed   [hihd] *v* fè atansyon
heel   [hihl] *n* talon
height   [hayt] *n* wotè
hell   [hèl] lanfè
help   [hèlp] *n* èd, asistans, *v* ede
hen   [henn] maman poul
her   [hèu] *prn* li
herb   [hèurb] *n* zepis

here [hihr] *adv* isit
herring [hèring] *n* aran
herself [hèuself] *prn* li-menm
hesitate [hesitet] *v* ezite
hiccup [hikòp] *n* okèt
hide [hayd] *n* po, *v* kache, sere
hideous [hidyous] *adj* lèd, efreyan
high [hay] *adj* wo, elve, apik
hijack [hayjak] *v* detounen
hill [hihl] *n* mòn
hire [hayèu] *v* enplwaye
hit [hit] *v* frape
hoarse [hòrs] anwe
hoe [ho] wou
hog [hòg] kochon
hold [hold] *v* kenbe
hole [hol] *n* twou
holiday [holodey] *n* konje
hollow [hòlow] *adj* kre
holy [holi] *adj* sen
home [hom] lakay
honest [honèst] *adj* onèt
honey [honni] *n* siwo
honor [honòr] *n* lonè
hoof [houf] *n* pat zannimo
hook [houk] *n* kwòk, zen, *v* kwoke

hope [hope] *n* lespwa, *v* espere
horn [hòrn] *n* kòn, klakxonn
hornet [hòrnèt] *n* gèp
horse [hòrs] *n* chwal, cheval
hospitality [hospitaliti] *n* ospitalite
host [host] *n* animatè, mètkay
hostess [hostès] *n* otès
hot [hat] *adj* cho
hotel [hotèl] lotèl
hour [hour] *n* lè
house [haws] *n* kay
how [haw] *adv* kijan, kòman
howl [hawl] *v* ranni
huge [hudj] *adj* gro {papa, manman}
human [humann] *adj* imen
humble [honmbl] *adj* modès
humid [houmid] *adj* imid, mouye
hundred [hanndred] *adj* san
hunger [hanngèu] *n* grangou
hunt [honnt] *n* lachas, *v* chase
hurry [hèuri] *v* kouri, prese
hurt [hèurt] *v* frape, maltrete
husband [hèusbannd] *n* mari
hush [hòch] silans
hyphen [hayfenn] tirè

I

ice   [ays] *n* glas
identify   [aydenntifay] *v* idantifye
idiot   [idyòt] *n* idyo
idle   [aydl] *adj* aryenafè
if   [if] *conj* si
ill   [ihl] *adj* malad
illegitimate   [iledjitimet] *adj* ilejitim, deyò
illicit   [ilisit] *adj* anbachal
image   [imedj] *n* imaj
imagination   [imajinechonn] *n* imajinasyon
imagine   [imadjin] *v* imajine
imbecile   [imbesil] *n* enbesil
imitate   [imitet] *v* imite
imitation   [imitechonn] *n* imitasyon
immediate   [imidyet] *adj* imedyat
immense   [imenns] *adj* imans, {manman, papa}
immoral   [imoral] *adj* imoral
immortal   [imòrtal] *adj* imòtèl
impart   [impart] *v* montre
impatient   [impachennt] *adj* enpasyan
impeach   [impitch] *v* anpeche, revoke

implicate   [impliket] *v* enplije
important   [impòrtent] *adj* enpòtan
impossible   [impòsobl] *adj* enposib
impress   [imprès] *v* enpresyone
improve   [improuv] *v* amelyore
in   [in] *prp* nan, andedan
inbred   [inbrèd] *adj* ras kabrit
inbreed   [inbrid] *v* akouple
incise   [insayz] *v* koupe
incite   [insayt] *v* ensite
inclination   [inklinechonn] *n* pant,
   enklinasyon
income   [inkòm] *n* salè
increase   [inkrihz] *n* ogmantasyon, *v*
   ogmante
incredible   [inkrehdibl] *adj* enkwayab
indeed   [indihd] *adv* kanmenm
ndependent   [indipendent] *adj* endepandan
indicate   [indiket] *v* endike, montre
indict   [indayt] *v* akize
indignation   [indignechonn] *n* endiyasyon
individual   [individyòl] *adj* grenn pa grenn,
   n oun
infect   [infèkt] *v* enfekte
infertile   [infèutayl] *adj* arid
influence   [influenns] *n* enfliyans

221

inherit   [inhèrit] *v* eritye
inheritance   [inheritanns] *n* eritaj
initial   [inichyal] *adj* inisyal, premye
ink   [ink] *n* lank
innocent   [inosent] *adj* inosan
inquire   [inkwayèu] *v* fè demann
insane   [insen] *adj* fou
insert   [insèurt] *v* foure
inside   [insayd] *n/adv* andedan
insist   [insist] *v* ensiste
insolent   [insolent] *adj* ensolan
instant   [instant] *adj* enstantane, *n* moman
instead   [instèd] *prp* olye
instruct   [instròkt] *v* montre
insult   [insòlt] *n* ensilt, *v* joure
intend   [intennd] *v* gen lentansyon
intent   [intennt] *n* lentansyon
interfere   [intèufihr] *v* entèfere
interrupt   [intèròpt] *v* entèronp
into   [intou] *prp* nan
introduce   [introdyous] *v* prezante
intrude   [introud] *v* deranje
invent   [invent] *v* envante
invisible   [invizibl] *adj* envizib
invite   [invayt] *v* envite
invoke   [invok] *v* envoke

iodine   [ayodayn] *n* yòd, {tentidyòd}
iron   [ayonn] *n* fè
irrigate   [iriget] *v* irige, awoze
irritate   [iritet] *v* irite
island   [aylend] *n* il, zile
it   [it] *prn* li
itch   [itch] *n* demanjezon, gratèl, *v* grate
itself   [itsèlf] *prn* li-menm

J

jab [djab] *v* koutpwen
jacket [djakèt] *n* jakèt, kostim
jag [djag] *v* dechikte
jam [djenm] *n* anbouteyaj
January [djanuari] *n* janvye
jar [djar] *n* bokal
jargon [djargonn] *n* jagon
jaw [djòw] *n* machwa
jealous [djalous] *adj* jalou
jelly [djèli] jele
jew [djouw] *adj* jwif
jewel [djouwèl] *n* bijou
job [djòb] *n* djòb, travay
jog [djòg] pouse
jogging [djògin] *n* djògin
join [djòyn] *v* rankontre, reyini, koud
joke [djok] *n* blag
jolly [djòli] *adj* kontan
journey [djòrni] *n* vwayaj
joy [djòy] *n* kontantman
judge [djòdj] *n* jij, *v* jije
jug [djòg] *n* krich

juice   [djyous] *n* ji
July   [djoulay] *n* jiyè
jump   [djonp] *v* ponpe, vole
June   [djyoun] *n* jen
junior   [djunyòr] *adj* jinyò
jury   [djyuri] *n* jiri
just   [djòst] *adj* jis, legal
justice   [djòstis] *n* lajistis, jistis
justify   [djòstifay] *v* jistifye

K

kangaroo   [kenngourou] *n* kangourou
karate   [keurate] *n* karate
keen   [kihn] *adj* fen, file, pike
keep   [kihp] *v* kenbe
key   [kih] *n* kle
kick   [kihk] *n* kou, *v* frape ak pye
kid   [kihd] *n* timoun
kidney   [kihdni] *n* ren {grenn vant}
kill   [kihl] *v* tiye, touye
killer   [kihlèu] *n* asasen
kin   [kin] paran
kind   [kaynd] *adj* janti
kindling   [kindling] *n* bwapen
king   [king] *n* wa
kink   [kink] *n* pli, ne
kiss   [kihs] *n* bo
kitchen   [kitchenn] *n* kizin, lakizin
kite   [kayt] *n* sèvolan, kap
kitten   [kitenn] *n* chat
knack   [nak] *n* talan
knave   [nev] *n* koken
knee   [ni] *n* jenou

knife   [nayf] *n* kouto
knit   [nit] *v* brode, trikote
knock   [nòk] *v* frape
knot   [nòt] *n* ne
know   [now] *v* konnen
knowledge   [nowlèdj] *n* konesans, save
known   [nown] *adj* rekoni
kola   [kola] *n* kola

L

labor   [lebèu] *n/v* travay, *n* doulè akouchman
lace   [les] *v* lase
lack   [lak] *n* mank, *v* manke
lad   [lad] *n* jennjan
ladle   [ladl] *n* louch
lady   [ledi] *n* madanm
lake   [lek] *n* lak
lamb   [lenmb] *n* mouton
land   [lennd] *n* tè, teren
landlord   [lennlòrd] *n* pwopriyetè
landscape   [lennskep] *n* peyizaj, jaden flè
lane   [len] *n* liy, bò lari
lapse   [laps] *n* defayans, erè, *v* perime
lard   [lard] *n* grès kochon, la
large   [lardj] *adj* laj
lash   [lach] *n* kout fwèt
lassitude   [lasityud] *n* kò kraze
last   [last] *adj* dènye
late   [let] *adj* anreta, *adv* ta
laugh   [lahf] *v* ri
law   [lòw] *n* lalwa, lwa, dwa
lawn   [lòwn] *n* gazon

lax [laks] *adj* neglijan, vag
lay [ley] *v* kouche, etann, blayi
lazy [lezi] *adj* parese
lead [lèd] *n* plon
lead [lid] *v* dirije, kòmande
leaf [lif] *n* fèy
leak [lik] *n* fuit
lean [lin] *v* panche, apiye
learn [lèurn] *v* aprann
lease [lis] *n* lwaye, *v* lwe
least [list] *adj* mwens, mwenn
leather [lèdvèu] *n* kui, tchwi
leave [liv] *v* kite, lese, pati, soti
leech [lich] *n* sansi, vantouz
leek [lik] *n* poro
left [lèft] *adj* gòch
leg [lèg] *n* pye
legible [ledjibl] *adj* lizib
leisure [lizyèur] *n* pastan, lwazi
lemon [lèmonn] *n* sitron
lend [lennd] *v* prete
length [lengf] *n* longè
less [lès] mwens
lesson [lèsonn] *n* leson
let's [lèts] *v* ann
letter [lètèu] *n* lèt

level [lèvèul] *n* nivo, *v* nivle

liar [layèu] *n* mantè, djòlè

lick [lick] niche, lanbe

lid [lid] *n* kouvèti, bouchon

lie [lay] *n* manti, boul

life [layf] *n* lavi, vi

lift [lift] *v* leve, monte

light [layt] *n* limyè, *adj* leje

lightning [laytning] *n* zeklè

like [layk] *adj* tankou, kon, *v* renmen

lime [laym] *n* lacho

line [layn] *n* liy

linen [linenn] *n* dra, lenn

link [link] *n* lyen, *v* relye

lion [layonn] *n* lyon

lip [lip] *n* pobouch, lèv

liquid [likwid] *n* likid

list [list] *n* lis

little [litl] *adj* piti, enpe

live [layv] *v* viv, abite, rete

liver [livèu] *n* fwa

lizard [lizard] *n* leza, zandolit

loaf [lof] *n* pen, *v* flannen

loan [loan] *n* anpren, *v* prete

local [lokòl] *adj* lokal, peyi, natif-natal

locate [loket] *v* lokalize, jwenn

lock [lòk] *n* kadna, *v* kadnase, bloke
lodge [lòdj] *n* lòj, *v* ebèje, bay ladesant
loft [lòft] *n* galata
log [lòg] *n* bout bwa
log [lòg] *n* jounal, dosye, *v* note
lone [lon] *adj* sèl
long [long] *adj* long
look [look] *n* rega, *v* gade
loop [loup] *n* riban, *v* anroule
loose [lous] *adj* branlan
lose [lous] *v* pèdi
loss [lòs] *n* pèt, chagren
lottery [loteri] *n* lotri
loud [lawd] *adj* fò
lousy [lawzi] *adj* degoutan
low [low] *adj* ba
lucid [lyusid] *adj* lisid, tèt klè
luck [lòk] *n* chans
lucre [lukèu] *n* magouyè
lug [lòhg] *v* trennen
lumber [lonmbèu] *n* bwa
lump [lonmp] *n* mas, gro moso
lunch [lohnch] *n* dine, manje midi
lure [lyur] *v* aleche, fè lasisiy
lust [lòst] *v* konvwate

M

machine   [machin] *n* machin, *v* fòme
mad   [mad] *adj* fache, fou
magic   [madjik] *adj* majik
magnificent   [magnifisent] *adj*
maid   [med] *n* bòn, restavèk
main   [men] *adj* prensipal, santral
maintain   [mennten] *v* mentni
maize   [mez] *n* mayi
major   [medjèu] *adj* prensipal, *n* majò
make   [mek] *n* mak, *v* fè
male   [mel] *adj* mal
malice   [malis] *n* malis
malign   [malign] *adj* nuizib
man   [man] *n* mesye, moun, nèg
manage   [manedj] *v* dirije, debouye
manifold   [manifold] *n* manifoul
mankind   [mennkaynd] *n* imanite, limanite
mansion   [mennchonn] *n* mansyon, gro kay
manual   [manual] *adj* manyèl, *n* liv
manufacture   [manufaktyèu] *n* fabrik,izin, *v* fabrike
manuscript   [manyuskript] *n* maniskri

many   [meni] *adj* anpil
map   [map] *n* kat
March   [martch] *n* mas
mark   [mark] *n* mak, tach, *v* make
market   [markèt] *n* mache
marriage   [maridj] *n* maryaj
marry   [mèri] *v* marye
marsh   [march] *n* marekaj
mash   [mach] *v* brase, kraze
match   [match] *n* alimèt, match, *v* matche
mate   [met] *n* matlo, *v* akouple
material   [matiryal] *adj* materyèl, *n* materyo
maternity   [matèuniti] *n* matènite
matter   [matèu] *n* matyè, problem
mature   [matchèur] *adj* mi, granmoun
May   [mey] *n* me
maybe   [meybi] *v* petèt
me   [mi] *prn* mwen
meadow   [mèdow] *n* preri
meal   [mihl] *n* manje, repa
mean   [mihn] *adj* move, fache, *n* mwayèn
meaning   [mihning] *n* siyifikasyon, sans
means   [mihns] *n* mwayen
measure   [mèjèu] *n* mezi, *v* mezire
meat   [mit] *n* vyann, chè
meet   [miit] *n* rankont, *v* rankontre

233

mellow [mèlow] *n* dou, jovyal

melt [mèlt] *v* fonn

member [menmbèu] *n* manm

menace [mènes] *n* menas

mend [mennd] *v* rapyese, rakomode

mental [menntal] *adj* mantal

mention [mennchonn] *v* mansyone

mercury [mèrkyuri] *n* mèki

mercy [mèursi] *n* pitye

mere [mihr] *adj* sèlman, *adv* apèn

merge [mèurdj] *v* fonn, amalgame

merit [merit] *n* merit, *v* merite

mess [mès] *n* fatra, dezòd

message [mèsedj] *n* mesaj

mettle [mètl] *n* kouraj

middle [midl] *adv* omilye, *n* mitan

might [mayht] *adv* petèt, *n* pisans

mild [mayld] *adj* mwayen, dous

milk [milk] *n* lèt

mince [mins] *v* rache, filange

mind [maynd] *n* lespri

mine [mine] *n* min, *prn* pa-m

minor [maynèu] *adj* minè

mint [mint] *n* mant

miracle [mirakl] *n* mirak

mirror [mirèu] *n* miwa, glas

misery [mizeuri] *n* mizè
misfortune [misfòtyoun] *n* malè
misguide [misgayd] *v* pedi
miss [mis] *v* manke
mist [mist] *n* labrim
mistake [mistek] *n* erè
mistress [mistrès] *n* metrès, (fanm) sou kote
mistrust [mistròst] *n* mefyans, *v* mefye
mix [miks] *n* melanj, *v* melanje
moan [mohn] *v* rale, jemi
mock [mòk] *v* moke
moderate [moderet] *adj/v* modere
modest [mòdèst] *adj* modès
moist [mòyst] *adj* imid, mouye
molest [mohlèst] *v* deranje, moleste
Monday [monndey] *n* lendi
money [mòni] *n* lajan, kòb
monger [monngèu] *n* pousè dife
monkey [monnki] *n* makak
monster [monnstèu] *n* mons
month [monnf] *n* mwa
mood [mouhd] *n* atmosfè, atitid
moon [mouhn] *n* lalin
more [mohr] *adj* plis, *adv* pi...pase
morning [mòrning] *n* maten
moss [mòs] *n* bab panyòl

most   [most] *adj* anpil, plis
moth   [mòtf] *n* papiyon lanp
mother   [mòdvèu] *n* manman
motion   [mochonn] *n* mouvman
mount   [mawnt] *n* mòn
mountain   [mawnten] *n* mòn, montay
mourn   [mohrn] *v* pote dèy
mouse   [maws] *n* sourit
moustache   [moustach] *n* moustach
mouth   [mawtf] *n* bouch
move   [mouv] *v* deplase
much   [mòtch] *adv* anpil
muck   [mòk] *n* fimye
mud   [mòd] *n* labou
mushroom   [mochroum] *n* chanpiyon,
  djondjon
must   [mòst] *v* dwe, *n* nesesite
mute   [myout] *adj* bèbè
mutton   [mòtonn] *n* mouton
mutual   [myoutual] *adj* resipwòk
my   [may] mwen
mysterious   [mistiryous] *adj* mistik

N

nail [neyl] *n* zong, klou, *v* kloure
naked [neked] *adj* toutouni
name [nem] *n* non, *v* nonmen
nap [nap] *n* kabicha
napkin [napkin] *n* sèvyèt
narrate [naret] *v* rakonte
narrow [narow] *adj* etwat
nasty [nasti] *adj* degoutan, dezagreyab,
    malpwòp
nation [nechonn] *n* nasyon
native [netiv] *adj* natif-natal
naughty [nòti] *adj* vakabon
near [nihr] *adv* toupre, akote, pre
neat [nit] *adj* pwòp
necessary [nesesari] *adj* nesesè
neck [nèk] *n* kou
need [nid] *n/v* bezwen
needle [nidl] *n* zegi, egui
neglect [neglèkt] *v* neglije
neighbor [nebòhr] *n* vwazen
neither [nidvèu] *adv* ni youn ni lòt, ni... ni
nephew [nèfyou] *n* neve

nest [nèst] *n* nich
never [nèvèu] *adv* jamè, janm
new [nyou] *adj* nouvo, nèf
news [nyouz] *n* nouvèl
next [nèkst] pwochen
nice [nays] bon, janti
niece [nihs] *n* nyès
nifty [nifti] *adj* debouya
night [nayt] *n* lanuit, nuit
nimble [nimbl] *adj* ajil
nine [nayn] *adj* nèf
nineteen [nayntin] *adj* diznèf
ninety [naynti] *adj* katrevendis
nip [nip] *v* zongle, koupe, kase boujon
no [no] non, *adj* okenn
nobody [nobòdi] *prn* pèsonn
nod [nòd] *v* souke tèt
node [nod] *n* ne
noise [nòyz] *n* bwi, bri
none [none] *prn* okenn
nonsense [nonnsenns] *n* nonsans
noon [noun] *n* midi
noose [nous] nekoulan
nor [nòr] *adv* ni
north [nòrtf] *n* direksyon nò, nan nò
nose [noz] *n* nen

nostril   [nostril] *n* twou nen, narin
not   [nòt] pa (negasyon)
note   [not] *n* nòt, *v* note
nothing   [nòtfing] *prn* anyen
notice   [notis] *n* avi, notis
notion   [nochonn] *n* nosyon
nourish   [nèurich] *v* nouri
novel   [nòvèl] *n* roman
November   [novenmbèu] *n* novanm
now   [naw] *adv* kounye-a
nowhere   [nowèhr] *adv* okenn kote
noxious   [nòkchyous] *adj* nosif
nuclear   [nukleyèu] *adj* nikleyè
nude   [nyoud] *adj* toutouni
nuisance   [nuizanns] *n* nizans
numb   [nonmb] *adj* ankiloze, dòmi
number   [nonmbèu] *n* nonm, chif
nun   [nonn] *n* relijyez, mamè, chèsè
nurse   [nèurs] *n* enfimyè, mis
nut   [nòt] *n* nwa, grenn

O

oak   [ok] *n* bwatchèn
oar   [òr] *n* zaviron
oat   [ot] *n* avwan
oath   [otf] *n* sèman
obedient   [obidyent] *adj* obeyisan
obese   [obis] *adj* obèz
obey   [obey] *v* obeyi
object   [obdjèkt] *n* objè, bagay
obligate   [obliget] *v* oblije
oblivious   [oblivyous] *adj* enkonsyan
obscene   [obsin] *adj* obsèn
obscure   [obskyour] *adj* fènwa
observe   [obsèurv] *v* obsève
obsess   [obsès] *v* obsede
obsolete   [obsolit] *adj* demode
obstacle   [obstakl] *n* obstak
obstinate   [obstinet] *adj* obstine
obstruct   [obstròkt] *v* bare, bouche
obtain   [obten] *v* pran, obteni
obvious   [obvyous] *adj* evedan, aklè
occasion   [okejyon] *n* okazyon
occupy   [òkupay] *v* okipe, pran

occur [okèur] *v* rive, pase
ocean [ochann] *n* loseyan
October [oktobèu] *n* oktòb
odd [òd] *adj* dròl, enpe
odor [odòr] *n* odè, lòdè
off [òf] *adj* etenn
offend [ofennd] *v* ofanse
offense [òfenns] *n* ofans
offer [òfèur] *v* ofri, *n* òf
office [òfis] *n* biwo, kabinè
officer [òfisèu] *n* ofisye, jandam
often [òfenn] *adv* souvan
oil [òyl] *n* luil, *v* luile
old [old] *adj* vye, aje
olive [òliv] *n* oliv
omen [omenn] *n* prezaj
on [onn] *adj* limen
once [wonns] *adv* onfwa, yon sèl fwa
one [wonn] *adj* youn, en
oneself [wonnsèlf] *prn* menm
onion [onyonn] *n* zonyon
only [onnli] *adv* sèlman, sèl
onto [ontou] *prp* sou
open [openn] *v* ouvri, louvri
opinion [opinyonn] *n* opinyon
opportunity [opòrtyouniti] *n* opòtinite

or [òr] *conj* oswa, oubyen, osinon
oral [oral] *adj* oral
orange [orandj] *n* zoranj
order [òrdèu] *n* lòd, kòmann, *v* kòmande
ordinary [òrdinèri] *adj* òdinè, banal
ore [òr] *n* minrè
origin [oridjin] *n* orijin
orphan [òrfann] *n* òfelen
other [òdvèu] *adj* lòt
our [awèur] *prn* nou
ours [awèurz] *prn* pa-n
out [awt] *n* deyò
outcome [awtkòm] *n* rezilta
outdated [awtdeted] *adj* demode
outlet [awtlèt] *n* sikisal
outlook [awtlouk] *n* pespektiv
outrageous [awtredjous] *adj* ekzòbitan
outside [awtsayd] *n* deyò
oven [ovenn] *n* fou
over [ovèu] *prp* anro, anlè
overcharge [ovèutchardj] *v* majore
overcoat [ovèukot] *n* padsi
overcome [ovèukòm] *v* venk, depase
overcrowd [overkrawd] *v* ankonbre
overdue [ovèudou] *adj* anreta
overflow [ovèuflow] *v* debòde

owe   [ow] *v* dwe
owl   [awl] *n* koukou
own   [own] *v* posede, genyen
ox   [òks] *n* bèf
oxtail   [òkstel] *n* ke bèf
oyster   [òystèu] *n* zuit

P

pace   [pes] *v* apante
pacific   [pasifik] *adj* pasifik
pack   [pak] *n* pake, koli *v* anpakte, anbale
padlock   [padlòk] *n* kadna
pain   [pen] *n* doulè
paint   [pent] *v* pentire, *n* penti
pair   [pèr] *n* pè, *adj* doub
palace   [palas] *n* palè
pale   [pel] *adj* pal
palm   [palm] *n* pye palmis, plamye
palsy   [palsi] *n* paralizi
pamper   [panmpèu] *v* dòlote
pan   [penn] *n* kasròl, bonm
pang   [penng] *n* doulè
panic   [panik] *n* panik, *v* panike
pantry   [penntri] *n* gadmanje
pants   [pents] *n* pantalon
paper   [pepèu] *n* papye
paradise   [paradayz] *n* paradi
parcel   [parsèl] *n* pakè, *v* separe tè
parch   [partch] *v* griye
parent   [perent *n* paran, fanmi

parley   [parley] *v* palmante, *n* poupale
parrot   [peròt] *n* jako
parsley   [parsli] *n* pèsi
part   [part] *n* moso, pyès
partake   [partek] *v* patisipe
participate   [partisipet] patisipe
particular   [partikyula] *adj* espesyal,
   patikilye
party   [parti] *n* pati, fèt
pass   [pas] *v* pase
passenger   [pasenndjèu] *n* pasaje
passion   [pachonn] *n* pasyon
past   [past] *n* lepase
pastry   [pestri] *n* patisri
patch   [patch] *n* patch, pyès, *v* patche,
   rakomode
patience   [pechenns] *n* pasyans
pattern   [patèurn] *n* modèl, egzanp, *v*
   modele
pauper   [pòpèur] *n* pòv, endijan
pavement   [pevment] *n* pave, asfalt
paw   [pòw] *n* pat, grif
pawn   [pòwn] *v* plannen
pay   [pey] *v* peye
pea   [pi] *n* pwa
peace   [pihs] *n* lapè

peach [pitch] *n* pèch
peak [pihk] *n* tèt, somè
pear [pèr] *n* pwar
peasant [pèzant] *n* peyizan, abitan
peck [pèk] *v* beke
peculiar [pekyular] *adj* spesifik
pedal [pèdal] *n* pedal, *v* pedale
peek [pihk] *v* gade vit
peel [pihl] *v* kale
peep [pihp] *v* fè jouda
peeve [pihv] *v* irite, anmède
pelt [pèlt] *v* kalonnen
pen [penn] *n* plim
pencil [pennsil] *n* kreyon
penetrate [penetret] *v* penetre, antre
people [pihpl] *n* moun, pèp
pepper [pèpèu] *n* pwav, piman
percent [pèusent] *n* pousantaj
perform [pèrfòrm] *v* egzekite, fè travay
perfume [pèufyoum] *n* pafen
perhaps [pèuhaps] *adv* petèt
peril [peril] *n* danje
perish [pèrich] *v* peri
permit [pèurmit] *n* lisans, pèmi, *v* pèmèt
perplex [pèurplèks] *adj* anbarase
persecute [pèursekyout] *v* pèsekite

persist [pèsist] *v* pèsiste
person [pèursonn] *n* moun
persuade [pèursuaed] *v* pèsuade
pet [pèt] *n* bèt kay
petrol [petrol] *n* petròl
pick [pik] *v* ranmase, pran, *n* pik
picture [piktyèu] *n* foto, *v* figire, imajine
pie [pay] *n* tat
piece [pihs] *n* moso, pyès, *v* kole
pierce [pihrs] *v* pèse
pig [pig] *n* kochon
pigeon [pidjonn] *n* pijon
pile [payl] *n* pil
pillar [pilar] *n* poto, pilye
pillow [pilo] *n* zorye
pimple [pinmpl] *n* bouton
pin [pin] *n* zepeng, *v* tache
pincers [pinsèurz] *n* pens
pinch [pinch] *v* zongle
pine [payn] *n* (pye) bwapen
pineapple [paynapl] *n* anana
pink [pink] *adj* roz
pipe [payp] *n* pip, tiyo, *v* kondi
pit [piht] *n* ravin, trou
pitcher [pitchèu] *n* krich
pity [piti] *n* pitye

place [ples] *n* kote, *v* mete
placebo [plasibo] *n* plasebo
placid [placid] *adj* trankil
plain [plen] *adj* klè, kare, *n* laplenn
plait [plet] *n* très, *v* trese, kòde
plant [plent] *n* plant
plate [plet] *n* asyèt, plat
play [ple] *v* jwe, *n* pyèsteyat
plea [pli] *n* plèd, jistifikasyon
plead [plid] *v* plede, enplore
pleasant [plèzant] *adj* amizan
please [pliz] *v* plè kontante; silvouple!,
    souple!
pleasure [plèjèu] *n* plezi
pledge [plèdj] *n* gaj, *v* garagti
plenty [plenti] *adj* ase, anpil
plot [plòt] *v* konplote, *n* pasèl, teren
pluck [plòk] *v* deplimen, rache, keyi
plug [plòg] *v* bouche, *n* priz kouran
plum [plonm] *n* prin
plump [plonmp] *adj* gra,
plunge [plonndj] *v* plonje
pneumonia [numonya] *n* nemoni
pocket [pòkèt] *n* pòch, *v* anpoche
point [pòynt] *v* montre, *n* pwen
poison [pòyzonn] *n* pwazon, *v* anpwazonnen

248

polite [polayt] *adj* poli, janti
poll [pol] *n* vòt, eleksyon
pond [ponnd] *n* basen
ponder [ponndèu] *v* reflechi
pool [poul] *n* pisin
poor [pour] *adj* pòv
pork [pòrk] *n* (vyann) kochon
porter [pòrtèu] *n* pòtè
possess [pozès] *v* posede
possibility [pòsibiliti] *n* posiblite
possibly [pòsibl, *adj* posib
post [post] *v* poste, *n* lapòs
post office [postòfis] *n* (biro) lapòs
postman [postmann] *n* faktè
postpone [postpon] *v* retade
pot [pòt] *n* po
potato [poteto] *n* pòmdetè
pour [por] *v* vide
poverty [pòvèuti] *n* povrete
powder [pawdèu] *n* poud
power [pawèu] *n* pisans, *v* alimante
praise [prez] *v* glorifye, *n* elòj
pray [pre] *v* priye
precaution [prikòchonn] *n* prekosyon
precede [prisid] *v* presede, vin anvan
precious [prèchous] *adj* presye, chè

precise   [prisayz] *adj* presi, egzak
predict   [predikt] *v* predi
preface   [prefes] *n* prefas
prefer   [prifèu] *v* prefere, pito
pregnant   [prègnant] *adj* ansent, gròs
prejudice   [predjudis] *n* prejije
prepare   [pripèr] *v* prepare
presence   [prezenns] *n* prezans
present   [prèzent] *adj* la, prezan
present   [prèzent] *n* kado
presently   [prèzantli] *adv* alèkile, kounye-a
preserve   [prizèurv] *v* prezève, *n* konfiti
press   [près] *v* peze, *n* laprès
pretend   [pritennd] *v* pretann
pretty   [priti] *adj* bèl
prevail   [privel] *v* domine
prevent   [privent] *v* prevni, evite
previous   [privyous] *adj* presedan
price   [prays] *n* pri
prick   [prik] *v* pike
pride   [prayd] *n* fyète
priest   [prist] *n* pè, prèt
primary   [praymèri] *adj* anpremye
print   [print] *v* enprime
prison   [prizonn] *n* prizon
private   [prayvet] *adj* prive

probable   [probebl] *adj* probab
proceed   [prosid] *v* kontinye
proceeds   [prosids] *n* benefis, montan
proclaim   [proklem] *v* proklame
procreate   [prokriyet] *v* prokreye, fè pitit
procure   [prokyur] *v* bay, fè jwenn
produce   [prodous] *n* danre, legim, *v* produi
professor   [profèsèu] *n* profesè
proffer   [profèu] *v* prezante
profit   [pròfit] *n* profi, *v* profite
profound   [profawnd] *adj* fon, byen panse
profuse   [profyouz] *adj* abondan
prohibit   [prohibit] *v* defann
prolong   [prolong] *v* prolonje
prominent   [prominent] *adj* repete, fò
promise   [pròmis] *n* promès, *v* promèt
promote   [promot] *v* avanse, monte grad
prompt   [pronpt] *adj* rapid
pronounce   [pronawns] *v* prononse
proof   [prouf] *n* prèv, *v* verifye
proper   [pròpèu] *adj* onèt, konvnab
property   [pròpèuti] *n* propriyete, byen
propose   [propoz] *v* propoze
prosper   [pròspèu] *v* prospere, rive, reyisi
protect   [protèkt] *v* proteje
protrude   [protroud] *v* leve, pouse, soti

proud [prawd] *adj* fyè
prove [prouv] *v* prouve
proverb [pròvèub] *n* provèb, diton
provide [provide] *v* founi
prowl [prwal] *v* rode
pub [pòb] *n* kafe, bistro
publish [pòblich] *v* pibliye
puff [pòf] *n* souf, *v* soufle
puke [pyouk] *v* vomi
pull [phoul] *v* rale
pulley [phouli] *n* pouli
pump [ponp] *n* ponp, *v* ponpe
punish [pònich] *v* pini, reprimande
punishment [pònichment] *n* pinisyon
pupil [pyoupil] *n* elèv
puppet [pòpèt] *n* poupe, mannken
purchase [pèuches] *n* acha
purify [pyourifay] *v* pirifye
purpose [pèurpos] *n* entansyon
purse [pèurs] *n* bous, *v* plise
pursue [pèursou] *v* pouswiv
push [pouch] *v* pouse
put [pout] *v* mete, depoze
puzzle [pòzl] *n* devinèt, problèm

Q

quadruple   [kwadrupl] *adj* kat fwa
quaint   [kwent] *adj* dròl
quake   [kwek] *n* tranbleman tè
qualm   [kwalm] *n* kèplen, noze
quantity   [kwanntiti] *n* kantite
quarrel   [kwarèl] *n* batay, goumen
quarry   [kwari] *n* karyè
quart   [kwart] *adj* onka, ka galon
quarter   [kwartèu] *n* katye, *adj* onka
quash   [kwach] *v* kraze, toufe
queen   [kwin] *n* rèn
quench   [kwennch] *v* etenn, tranpe
question   [kwestchonn] *n* kesyon, *v* kesyone
quick   [kwik] *adj* vit, rapid
quiet   [kwayèt] *adj* trankil
quilt   [kwilt] *n* kouvèti, lenn
quit   [kwit] *v* kite, lage
quite   [kwayt] *adv* ase, anverite
quiz   [kwiz] *n* egzamen

R

rabbit   [rabit] *n* lapen
race   [res] *n* kous, *v* fè kous
race   [res] *n* ras, rasmoun
rack   [rak] *n* etajè
radiator   [redyetèu] *n* radyatè
radish   [radich] *n* radi
rag   [rag] *n* ranyon
ragamuffin   [ragmòfin] *n* sanzave
rage   [redj] *n* raj
ragged   [ragd] *adj* dechikte
raid   [red] *n* atak, razya
rail   [rel] *n* baro, parapè
rain   [ren] *n* lapli
raise   [rez] *v* leve, drese, kanpe
rally   [rali] *n* raliman, *v* rasanble
ramble   [renmbl] *v* divage
ramp   [ranp] *n* ranp
rancid   [rannsid] *adj* ransi
random   [ranndonm] *adj* (o) aza
range   [renndj] *n* pòte, direksyon, *v* aliyen, klase
rank   [rank] *n* grad

ransack [rennsak] *v* devalize
ransom [rennsonm] *n* ranson
rap [rap] *v* frape
rape [rep] *v* vyole
rapid [rapid] *adj* rapid, vit
rapt [rapt] *adj* anchante, antouzyas
rare [rèr] *adj* ra, *n* vyann kri
rarely [rèrli] *adv* raman
rascal [raskal] *n* koken
rash [rach] *adj* enpridan
rasp [rasp] *v* kòche, rape
rat [rat] *n* rat
rate [ret] *n* pousantaj, to
rather [radvèu] *adv* pito
ration [reconn] *n* rasyon
ravage [ravedj] *n* ravaj, *v* devaste, ravaje
rave [rev] *n* elòj, *v* divage, tanpete
ravel [ravèl] *v* mele, anbouye
raven [revenn] *n* kaw, boustabak
ravish [ravich] *v* dapiyan, vyole
raw [ròw] *adj* kri
ray [rey] *n* reyon
raze [rez] *v* demantle
razor [rezò] *n* razwa
reach [ritch] *v* atenn, rive
read [rihd] *v* li, fè lekti

ready   [redi] *adj* pare *v* prepare
real   [riyal] *adj* reyèl, tout bon
rear   [rhir] *n* dèyè, *v* elve, drese
reason   [rizonn] *n* rezon, *v* rezone, reflechi
reassure   [riasyur] *v* rasire
rebellion   [ribèlyonn] *n* rebelyon
rebuke   [ribyouk] *v* reprimande, rele sou
receive   [risiv] *v* resevwa
recent   [risent] *adj* resan
recess   [risès] *n* rekreyasyon
recognize   [rikognayz] *v* rekonèt
recommend   [rèkomannd] *v* rekòmande
record   [rèkòd] *n* dosye, *v* enskri
recover   [rikovèu] *v* repran, rejwenn
red   [rèd] *adj* rouj, wouj
reduce   [ridous] *v* redui, amensi
reek   [rihk] *n* charony, *v* santi move
reel   [rihl] *n* bobin, *v* bobine
refer   [rihfèu] *v* refere
refrigerator   [refridjeretèu] *n* frijidè
refuse   [rèfyouz] *n* fatra
refuse   [rifyouz] *v* refize
regard   [rigard] *n* rega, koutje, *v* gade,
  konsidere
region   [ridjyonn] *n* rejyon, zòn
regret   [rigrèt] *n* chagren, *v* regrete

reject [ridjèkt] *n* rejè, *v* refize, rejete
relate [rilet] *v* rakonte, relate
relative [rèlativ] *n* paran, fanmi
relax [rihlaks] *v* rilaks, detann
release [rilis] *n* liberasyon *v* lage, libere
relief [rilif] *n* soulajman, alemye
relish [rèlich] *n* gou, asezonman
rely [rilay] *v* depann sou, gen konfyans
remain [rimehn] *n* restan, *v* rete
remark [rimark] *n* remak, *v* remake
remedy [rèmedi] *n* remèd, *v* soulaje, swaye
remember [rimenmbèu] *v* sonje
remind [remaynd] *v* raple, fè sonje
remission [remichonn] *n* konvalesans
remit [remit] *v* remèt
remorse [rimòrs] *n* remò
remote [rimot] *adj* adistans, lwen
remove [rimouv] *v* retire, wete
render [rendèu] *v* remèt, rann, tradui (lang)
rent [rent] *n* lwaye, *v* lwe
repair [ripèr] *v* ranje, repare
repeat [ripiht] *v* repete
resist [rezist] *v* reziste
respect [rispèkt] *n* respè, *v* respekte
respond [risponnd] *v* reponn
response [risponns] *n* repons

rest   [rèst] *v* repoze, rete *n* restan

restrict   [restrikt] *v* restrenn

return   [ritèurn] *v* (voye) tounen, retounen

reveal   [rivihl] *v* revele, devwale, gaye (nouvèl)

revenge   [rivenndj] *n* revanch, revanj

review   [rivyou] *n* revi, revizyon, *v* repase

revise   [rivayz] *v* korije

reward   [riward] *n* rekonpans, *v* rekonpanse

rib   [rib] *n* kòt, zokòt

ribbon   [ribonn] *n* riban

rice   [rays] *n* diri

rich   [ritch] *adj* rich

rid   [rid] *v* debarase

riddle   [ridl] *n* devinèt

ride   [rayd] *v* monte (machin, chwal)

ridicule   [ridikyoul] *adj* bèt, ridikil

rifle   [rayfl] *n* fizi

right   [rayt] *adj* dwat, *adv* adwat

rigid   [ridjid] *adj* rèd, rijid, sèk

rind   [raynd] *n* po, krout

ring   [ring] *n* bag

rinse   [rins] *v* rense

riot   [rayòt] *n* atroupman

ripe   [rayp] mi, apwen

rise   [rayz] *v* leve kanpe

river   [rivèu] *n* rivyè, flèv, dlo
roach   [rotch] *n* ravèt
road   [rohd] *n* chemen, rout
roar   [rohr] *v* gronde, ranni
roast   [rohst] *v* boukannen, griye
rob   [ròb] *v* vole, vòlè
robber   [ròbèu] *n* vòlè
rock   [ròk] *n* ròch, galèt, *v* balanse, dodinen
rod   [ròd] *n* baton
rogue   [rog] *n* vakabon, vòlè
roll   [rol] *v* roule, *n* roulo
romance   [romanns] *n* romans
roof   [rouf] *n* tèt kay, twakay
room   [roum] *n* chanm
root   [rout] *n* rasin
rope   [rop] *n* kòd
rose   [roz] *n* roz
rot   [ròt] *n* pouriti, *v* pouri
rotten   [ròtenn] *adj* pouri
rough   [ròf] *adj* brital
round   [rawnd] *adj* ron, won *v* arondi
rouse   [rawz] *v* reveye
route   [rawt] *n* rout, *v* achemine
rove   [rov] *v* flannen
row   [row] *n* ranje, ran, *v* rame
rub   [ròb] *v* frote, masaje

rubber   [ròbèu] *n* kaoutchou
rubbish   [ròbich] *n* fatra
rude   [roud] *adj* grosoulye, grosye
ruin   [rouin] *n* ruin, *v* ruine
rule   [roul] *n* règ, *v* dirije, kòmande
rum   [ronm] *n* ronm
rumor   [roumèu] *n* bri, chuichui
run   [ronn] *v* kouri
rush   [ròch] *v* kouri prese, *n* bouskilad
rust   [ròst] *n* rouy, *v* rouye
rusty   [ròsti] *adj* rouye

S

sack [sak] *n* sak
sacrifice [sakrifays] *n* sakrifis
sad [sad] *adj* tris
safe [sef] *adj* senesòf, *n* kòfrefò
sail [seyl] *n* vwal, *v* navige
salad [salad] *n* salad
salary [salari] *n* salè
sale [sel] *n* lavant
saliva [selayva] *n* krache
salmon [sòlmonn] *n* somon
salt [sòlt] *n* sèl
salute [salyout] *v* salye
same [sem] *adj* menm
sample [senmpl] *n* echantiyon
sand [scnnd] *n* sab
sandwich [senndwitch] *n* sandwich
sane [sen] *adj* lisid
sash [sach] *n* sentiwon
satisfy [satisfay] *v* satisfè
saturate [satyuret] *v* satire, boure
Saturday [satèurde] *n* samdi
sauce [sos] *n* sòs

saucer   [sòsèur] *n* soukoup
sausage   [sòsedj] *n* sosis
savage   [savedj] *adj/n* sovaj
save   [sev] *v* sove
savior   [sevyòr] *n* sovè, lesovè
savor   [sevèu] *n* gou
say   [sey] *v* di
scald   [skòld] *v* chode
scale   [skel] *n* balans
scare   [skèr] *v* efreye, alame, fè pè
scent   [sent] *n* sant, odè
schedule   [skedyoul] *n* orè,
school   [skoul] *n* lekòl
science   [syanns] *n* syans
scissors   [sizòrz] *n* sizo
scold   [skold] *v* reprimande
scorch   [skòrtch] *v* rousi, boule
score   [skòr] *n* skò
scorn   [skòrn] *v* meprize
scoundrel   [skawndrèl] *n* kannay
scrape   [skrep] *v* grate, rafle
scratch   [skratch] *v* grafouyen
scream   [skrim] *v* rele [anmwe]
screen   [skrin] *n* ekran
screw   [skrou] *n* vis, boulon
scribble   [skribl] *v* madjigridji

scrub [skròb] *v* frote
sea [si] *n* lanmè, loseyan
seal [sihl] *n* tanpon, *v* sele
search [sèurtch] *v* chèche
seat [siht] *n* chèz
second [sèkonnd] *adj* dezyèm, *n* segonn
secret [sikrèt] *n* sckrè
secure [sekyour] *adj* ansekirite
sedate [sedet] *v* andòmi
seduce [sedous] *v* sedui
see [si] *v* wè
seed [sid] *n* grenn
seek [sik] *v* chèche
seem [sim] *v* sanble
seize [siz] *v* sezi
select [selèkt] *v* seleksyone, chwazi
self [sèlf] *n* tèt, kò
selfish [sèlfich] *adj* egoyis
sell [sèl] *v* vann
send [sennd] *v* voye
sense [senns] sans
sensible [sennsibl] *adj* sansib
sentence [senntens] *n* fraz
separate [sèpret] *adj* apa, separe, *v* separe
September [septenmbèu] *n* septanm
sequel [sekwèl] *n* fen, suit

sequence   [sekwenns] *n* sekans
serious   [siryous] *adj* serye
serpent   [sèurpent] *n* koulèv
servant   [sèurvant] *n* restavèk, bòn
serve   [sèurv] *v* sèvi
service   [sèurvis] *n* sèvis
settle   [sètl] *v* etabli, tabli
seven   [sèvenn] *adj* sèt
seventy   [sèvennti] *adj* swasanndis
several   [sèvral] *adj* plizyè
severe   [sevir] *adj* sevè
sew   [so] *v* koud
sex   [sèks] *n* sèks
shabby   [chabi] *n* ranyon
shade   [ched] *n* lonbraj
shadow   [chado] *n* lonbraj
shake   [chek] *v* souke
shallow   [chalo] *n* pa fon
shame   [chem] *n* ront, dezonè
shape   [chep] *n* fòm
share   [chèr] *v* separe, pataje
sharp   [charp] *adj* file, pwenti
shave   [chev] *v* fè bab, raze
she   [chi] *prn* li
sheep   [chip] *n* mouton
sheet   [chiht] *n* dra

shelf   [chèlf] *n* etajè
shell   [chèl] *n* koki
shelter   [chèltèu] *n* ladesant, tonnèl
shift   [chift] *v* chanje
shine   [chayn] *v* klere
ship   [chip] *n* bato
shirt   [chèurt] *n* chemiz
shiver   [chivèu] *v* tranble (fredi)
shock   [chòk] *n* chok, *v* choke
shoe   [chou] *n* soulye
shoot   [chout] *v* tire
shop   [chòp] *n* magazen, boutik, *v* achte
shore   [chòr] *n* bòdmè
short   [chòrt] *n* chòt, bout kanson
shoulder   [choldèu] *n* zepòl, *v* sipòte
shout   [chawt] *v* rele (pale) fò
show   [cho] *v* montre, *n* program
shower   [chawèu] *n* douch
shrink   [chrink] *v* retresi
shut   [chòt] *v* fèmen
shy   [chay] *adj* timid
sick   [sik] *adj* malad
side   [sayd] *n* bò, kote
sign   [sayn] *n* siy, *v* siyen
signature   [signatchèu] *n* siyati
silence   [saylanns] *n* silans

silk   [slik] *n* swa
silly   [sili] *adj* enbesil, bèt, komik
silver   [silvèu] *n* ajan, lajan
similar   [simila] *adj* sanble, genlè menm
simple   [simpl] *adj* senp
sin   [sin] *n* peche
since   [sins] *adv* depi
sincere   [sinsir] *adj* sensè
single   [singl] *adj* selibatè, grenn
sink   [sink] *v* plonje, koule
sip   [sip] *v* sirote
sister   [sistèu] *n* sè
sit   [sit] *v* chita
six   [siks] *adj* sis
size   [sayz] *n* grosè, dimansyon
skate   [sket] *v* monte paten
skew   [skyou] *adj* krochi
skill   [skil] *n* talan
skin   [skin] *n* po
skirt   [skèurt] *n* jip
sky   [skay] *n* syèl
slack   [slak] *n* pantalon, kanson
slander   [slenndèu] *v* kalomnye
slang   [slenng] *n* jagon
slap   [slap] *v* souflete *n* kalòt
sleek   [slik] *adj* swa, dous

sleep [slip] *v* dòmi
sleeve [sliv] *n* manch
slice [slays] *n* tranch
slide [slayd] *v* glise
slightly [slaytly] *adv* toupiti
slim [slim] *adj* mens
sling [sling] *n* echap, *v* voye
slip [slip] *v* glise
slow [slo] *adj* dousman
sluggard [slògèud] *adj* parese
sly [slay] *adj* rize, sounwa
small [smòl] *adj* piti
smart [smart] *adj* fò, entelijan
smash [smach] *v* kraze
smell [smèl] *v* santi, pran odè
smile [smayl] *v* souri
smoke [smok] *v* fimen, *n* lafimen
smooth [smoutf] *adj* lis
smother [smòdvèu] *v* trangle, toufe
smoulder [smoldèu] *v* mijote, konsonmen
snack [snak] *n* goute
snail [snel] *n* kalmason
snake [snek] *n* koulèv
sneeze [sniz] *v* etènye
snore [snòr] *v* ronfle
snout [snawt] *n* djòl, machwè

snow [sno] *n* lanèj

so [so] *adv* alò, sitèlman, otan

soak [sok] *v* tranpe

soap [sop] *n* savon, *v* savonnen

sob [sòb] *v* kriye

society [sosayti] *n* sosyete, lasosyete

sock [sòk] *n* chosèt

soft [sòft] *adj* mou

soil [sòyl] *v* sal

soldier [sòldyèu] *n* solda

solemn [sòlèm], *adj* solanèl

solid [sòlid] *adj* fèm, solid

solution [solyuchonn] *n* solisyon, tranpe

solve [sòlv] *v* rezoud

somber [sonmbèu] *adj* sonm

some [sonm] *adj* enpe, kèk

somebody [sonmbòdi] *prn* yon moun

somehow [sonmhaw] *adv* enpòt kijan

something [sonmtfing] *n/prn* bayay

son [sonn] *n* pitit gason

son-in-law [soninlò] *n* bofis

soon [soun] *adv* talè

sore [sòr] *adj* kòkraz

sorrow [soro] *n* chagren

sorry [sòri] *v* regrèt

soul [sol] *n* nanm

sound [sawnd] *n* son
soup [soup] *n* soup, lasoup
sour [sawèu] *adj* si
south [sawtf] *n* sid, nansid
sow [so] *v* simen
space [spes] *n* plas, espas
spare [spèr] *adj* derechany
sparkle [sparkl] *v* klere
speak [spik] *v* pale
spectacle [spektakl] *n* spektak, program
speed [spid] *n* vitès
spend [spend] *v* depanse
spice [spays] *n* zepis
spider [spaydèu] *n* zariyen
spill [spil] *v* devide
spinster [spinstèu] *n* vyèyfi
spirit [spirit] *n* lespri, move zè
spit [spit] *v* krache
split [split] *v* separe
spoil [spòyl] *v* gate
spoon [spoun] *n* kiyè
spot [spòt] *n* tach
spread [sprèd] *v* gaye
spring [spring] *n* resò, prentan
square [skwèr] *adj* kare
squash [skwach] *n* joumou, kalbas, *v* kraze

stage [stedj] *n* etap
stair [stèr] *n* eskalye
stammer [stamèu] *v* bege
stamp [stenp] *n* tenm, *v* tenbre
stand [stennd] *v* kanpe, *n* etanda
star [star] *n* etwal, zetwal
stare [stèr] *v* fikse, gade fix
start [start] *v* stat
starve [starv] *v* grangou, mouri grangou
state [stet] *n* leta, *v* deklare
station [stechonn] *v* stasyon
stay [ste] *v* rete
steady [stèdi] *adj* fiks
steal [stil] *v* vole, vòlè
steam [stim] *n* vapè
steel [stil] *n* asye
step [stèp] *n* pa, mach
stew [stou] *n* bouyon
stick [stik] *n* baton
still [stil] *n* gildiv
stingy [stindji] *adj* kripya
stocking [stòking] *n* ba
stomach [stonmak] *n* vant, anbativant
stone [ston] ròch
stool [stoul] *n* taboure
stop [stòp] *n* stop, *v* estope

store [stòr] *n* boutik, magazen
storm [stòrm] *n* van, move tan
story [stòri] *n* istwa
straight [stret] *adj* dwat
strain [stren] *v* fòse
strange [strennj] *adj* dròl
strangle [strangl] *v* trangle
straw [strò] *n* pay, chalimo
stream [strim] *n* sousdlo, rivyè
street [strit] ri, lari
strength [strenktf] *n* fòs, kouraj
stress [strès] *n* tansyon
stretch [strètch] *v* rale
strict [strikt] *adj* strik
strike [strayk] *v* frape
string [sting] *n* fisèl, kòd
strong [strong] *adj* gen kouraj
struggle [strògl] *n* batay, lit, *v* lite
study [stèudi] *v* etidye
stupid [stoupid] *adj* estipid
subject [sòbdjèkt] *n* sijè
submit [sòbmit] *v* soumèt, remèt
subscribe [sòbskrayb] *v* abòne, souskri
suburb [sèubèurb] *n* fobou
success [sèuksès] *n* siksè
such [sèutch] *adj* kalite, tèl

suck [sòk] *v* souse
suddenly [sèudennli] *adv* sanzatann
suffer [sòfèu] *v* soufri
sugar [chouga] *n* sik
suggest [sèugjèst] *v* sijere
suicide [sousayd] *n* sisid, *v* siside
suit [sout] *n* kostim, *v* byen tonbe, fè prosè
sullen [sòlenn] *adj* mòksis
summer [sòmmèu] *n* ete, lete
summon [sòmonn] *v* konvoke
sun [sonn] *n* solèy, sole
Sunday [sunnde] *n* dimanch
sunflower [sonnflawèu] *n* flè solèy
superior [supiryò] *adj* siperyè
supply [suplay] *v* founi
support [supòrt] *v* sipòte, soutni
suppose [supoz] *v* sipoze
sure [chyour] *adj* sèten, si, asire
surface [sèurfes] *n* anlè
surgeon [sèurdjonn] *n* chirijyen
surprise [sèurprayz] *n* sipriz
surrender [surenndèu] *v* baylegen
surround [surawnd] *v* ansèkle
survive [sèuvayv] *v* siviv, chape
suspect [sèuspèkt] *adj* sispèk, *v* sispekte
suspend [suspennd] *v* sispann

suspicion   [suspichonn] *n* sispisyon
swallow   [swalo] *v* vale
sweat   [swèt] *v* sue, swe
sweep   [swip] *v* bale
sweet   [swit] *adj* dous, sikrè
swell   [swèl] *adj/v* anfle
swift   [swift] *adj* rapid
swim   [swim] *v* naje
swine   [swayn] *n* kochon
swing   [swing] *n* balansin, *v* balanse
switch   [switch] *n* switch, *v* chanje, pase
syllable   [silebl] *n* silab
syringe   [sirinj] *n* sereng

T

table   [tebl] *n* tab
tail   [teyl] *n* lake, ke
tailor   [telèu] *n* tayè
take   [tek] *v* pran
tale   [tel] *n* istwa, kont
talk   [tòk] *v* pale, koze, *n* koze
tall   [tòl] *adj* ro
tame   [tem] *v* donte
tangle   [tengl] *v* mele
tap   [tap] *v* tape
tape   [tep] *v* tep
tape recorder   [teprikòdèu] *n* tep
target   [targèt] *v* vize
tart   [tart] *adj* brak
task   [task] *n* travay
taste   [test] *n* gou, *v* goute
tax   [taks] *n* taks
tea   [ti] *n* te
teach   [titch] *v* montre, anseye
team   [tim] *n* ekip
tear   [tear] *v* dechire
tease   [tiz] *v* toumante

tedious   [tidyous] *adj* fatigan
teenager   [tinedjèu] *n* tinedjè
tell   [tèl] *v* rakonte, di
temper   [tenmpèu] *n* tanperaman
tempest   [tenmpèst] *n* tanpèt
temple   [tenmpl] *n* tanp
tempt   [tenpt] *v* tantc
ten   [tenn] *adj* dis
tenant   [tènant] *n* lokatè
tender   [tenndèu] *adj* tann, sansib
tense   [tenns] *adj* enève, rèd
tent   [tent] *n* tant
term   [tèurm] *n* tèm
terrible   [tèribl] *adj* terib
terror   [tèrèu] *n* laterè
test   [tèst] *n* tès, egzamen
thank   [tfenk] *v* remèsye
they   [dve] *prn* yo
thick   [tfik] *adj* epè
thief   [tfif] *n* vòlè
thigh   [tfay] *n* kuis
thin   [tfin] *adj* fen
thing   [tfing] *n* bagay
think   [tfink] *v* reflechi, panse
thirteen   [tfèutin] *adj* trèz
thirty   [tfèurti] *adj* trant

thought [tfòt] *n* panse
thousand [tfawzann] *adj* mil
thread [tfrèd] *n* fil
threat [tfrèt] *n* menas, *v* menase
three [tfri] *adj* twa
throat [tfrot] *n* gòj
throw [tfro] *v* voye
thumb [tfonm] *n* pous
thunder [tfonndèu] *n* loray
Thursday [tfèursde] *n* jedi
ticket [tikèt] *n* tikè
tidy [taydi] *adj* pwòp
tie [tay] *n* kravat, *v* mare
tighten [taytenn] *v* sere
till [till] *adv* jis, jiska
timber [timbèu] *n* bwa chapant
time [taym] *n* lè, tan
timid [timid] *adj* timid, kazwèl
tiny [tayni] *adj* toupiti
tire [tayèu] *v* fatige
tissue [tichyou] *n* papye twalèt
title [taytl] *n* tit
today [toude] *n* jodi
toe [to] *n* zòtèy
together [tougèdvèu] *adv* ansanm
toil [tòyl] *v* travay di, trimen

276

tomato   [tometo] *n* tomat
tomb   [tonm] *n* tonm
tomorrow   [toumoro] *n* demen
tongue   [tong] *n* lang
tonight   [tounayt] *n* aswè
too   [tou] *adv* tou, trò
tool   [toul] *n* zouti
tooth   [toutf] *n* dan
top   [tòp] *n* tèt
torch   [tòtch] *n* tòch
tortoise   [tòtòyz] *n* tòti
torture   [tòtchèu] *v* malmennen
total   [total] *n* total
touch   [tòtch] *v* touche, manyen
tough   [tòf] *adj* rèd
towel   [tawèul] *n* sèvyèt
town   [tawn] *n* vil, lavil
toy   [tòy] *n* jwèt
trace   [tres] *v* trase, *n* tras
track   [trak] *v* suiv
trade   [tred] *n* metye
traffic   [trafik] *n* trafik
train   [trenn] *n* tren
traitor   [tretèu] *n* trèt
transfer   [transfèu] *v* transfere, *n* tansfè
translate   [translet] *v* tradui

trash   [trach] *n* fatra, *v* tòchonnen
travel   [travèul] *n* vwayaj, *v* vwayaje
treasure   [trèjèu] *n* trezò
treat   [trit] *v* trete
tree   [trhi] *n* pyebwa
tremble   [trenmbl] *v* tranble
trim   [trim] *v* bòdi
trip   [trip] *n* vwayaj
trouble   [tròbl] *n* problèm, troub, *v* trouble
trousers   [trawzèuz] *n* pantalon
true   [trou] *n* vre
trunk   [tronk] *n* kòf
trust   [tròst] *v* fè konfyans
truth   [troutf] *n* laverite, verite
try   [tray] *v* eseye
Tuesday   [tyousde] *n* madi
turkey   [tèurki] *n* kodenn
turn   [tèurn] tounen, vire
tutor   [tutèur] *n* profesè
twelve   [twèlv] *adj* douz
twenty   [twennti] *adj* ven
twice   [tways] *adv* defwa
twin   [twin] *n* jimo
twist   [twist] *v* tòde
two   [tou] *adj* de

U

ugly [ògli] *adj* lèd
umbrella [onmbrèla] *n* parapli
unable [onnebl] *adj* enkapab
unbearable [onnbèrebl] *adj* ensipòtab
uncle [onnkl] *n* tonton, monnonk
uncommon [onnkòmonn] *adj* estraòdinè
unconscious [onnkonchous] *adj* san
  konesans
under [onndèu] *prp* anba
undergo [onndèugo] *v* sibi
underground [onndèugrawnd] *n* anbatè
understand [onndèustennd] *v* konprann
undo [onndou] *v* defè
uneven [onnivenn] *adj* inegal, ansibreka
unfortunately [onnfòtyounetli] *adv*
  malerezman
unhappy [onnhapi] *adj* tris, pa kontan
unify [younifay] *v* inifye
union [younyonn] *n* inyon, maryaj, sendika
unit [younit] *n* inite, grenn
unite [younayt] *v* ini, mare
until [onntil] *prp* jis (jouk), jiska, jiskaske

up   [òp] *adv* anlè, anro, soutèt
up-to-date   [òptoudet] *adj* resan, ajou
upset   [òpsèt] *adj* fache, deranje, trouble
urge   [èurdj] *v* ankouraje, rekòmande
us   [òs] *prn* nou
use   [youz] *v* itilize
used   [youzd] *adj* ize, dokazyon, dezyèm
   men
useful   [youzfoul] *adj* itil
usual   [youjuòl *adj* òdinè, selon lizaj
utensil   [youtennsil] *n* istansil
utility   [youtiliti] *n* itilite
utterance   [èuteranns] *n* espresyon

V

vacation [vekechonn] *n* vakans
vagabond [vagabonnd] *adj* eran, *n*
  vakabon, voryen
vague [veg] *adj* vag, raz
vain [ven] *adj* chèlbè
valiant [valyant] *adj* vanyan
valise [valiz] *n* valiz
valley [valey] *n* savann, plato
value [valyou] *n* valè
valve [valv] *n* valv
vanilla [vanila] *n* vaniy
vanish [vanich] *v* disparèt
vanquish [vennkwich] *v* venk, genyen
vapor [vepèu] *n* vapè
various [varyous] *adj* divès
varnish [varnich] *adj/v* vèni
vary [vari] *n* varye
vast [vast] *adj* vast
vegetable [vedjtebl] *n* legim
vehicle [vihikl] *n* machin
vend [vennd] *v* vann
venerate [veneret] *v* venere, respekte

venture   [venntyèu] *n* negòs, antrepriz, *v* riske

verdict   [vèudikt] *n* desizyon, jijman

vermin   [vèumin] *n* parazit, vèmin

verse   [vèus] *n* vè

very   [very] *adj* anpil, trè

vex   [vèks] *v* vekse

vice versa   [vaysevèusa] *adv* ale pou vini

vice   [vays] *n* vis, mani

victim   [viktim] *n* viktim

victory   [viktori] *n* viktwa

view   [vyou] *v* egzamine

village   [viledj] *n* bouk, vilaj

vinegar   [vinega] *n* vinèg

violate   [vayolet] *v* vyole, dezobeyi

violet   [vayolèt] *adj* vyolèt

virgin   [vèurdjin] *adj* tifi, vyèj

vision   [vijonn] *n* vizyon

vital   [vaytal] *adj* vital, serye

vocabulary   [vokabyoulèri] *n* vokabilè

vogue   [vog] *n* lamòd

voice   [vòys] *n* vwa, *v* prononse

volume   [vòlyoum] *n* volim

volunteer   [voluntir] *n* volontè

vomit   [vòmit] *n* vomi

vote   [vot] *n* vòt, *v* vote

voyage   [vòyadj] *n* vwayaj

W

wade [wed] *v* patoje
wage [wedj] *n* salè, peròl
wager [wedjèu] *n* paryaj, *n* parye
wail [weyl] *v* jemi
waist [west] *n* ren, tay
wait [wet] *v* tann
wake [wek] *n* veye, *v* reveye
walk [wòk] *v* mache, *n* demach
wall [wòl] *n* mi, panno
wallet [wòlèt] *n* bous
wander [wanndèu] *v* flannen
wane [wen] *n* dekadans, *v* tonbe
want [want] *v* vle
war [wòr] *n* lagè
ward [wòrd] *v* pare, detounen
warm [wòrm] *adj* tyèd
warn [wòrn] *v* prevni, avèti
warrant [wòrant] *n* manda, chèk, *v* garanti
wash [wach] *v* lave, *n* lesiv
wasp [wasp] *n* gèp
waste [west] *n* gaspiyaj, *v* gaspiye
watch [watch] *n* mont, *v* gade, siveye

water   [watèu] *n* dlo
wave   [wev] *n* vag, *v* flote
way   [wey] *n* chemen
we   [wi] *prn* nou
weak   [wik] *adj* fèb
wealth   [wèltf] *n* fòtin, byen
weapon   [wèponn] *n* zam
wear   [wèr] *v* pote, mcte
weather   [wèdvèu] *n* klima, tan
weave   [wiv] *v* tise, mare
web   [wèb] *n* filareye
wedding   [wèding] *n* maryaj
Wednesday   [wensde] *n* mèkredi
weed   [wid] *n* raje
week   [wik] *n* semèn, senmenn
weep   [wip] *v* kriye
weigh   [wey] *v* peze
weight   [weyt] *n* pwa
welcome   [wèlkòm] *n* bèlantre
welfare   [wèlfèr] *n* byennèt
well   [wèl] *n* sous, pui/pi, *adv* byen
west   [wèst] *n* lwès, nan lwès
wet   [wèt] *adj* mouye
whale   [wehl] *n* balèn
wharf   [warf] *n* waf
what   [wat] (*interr.*) kisa

whatever [watèvèu] *prn* nenpòt, kèlkeswa
wheat [wiht] *n* ble
wheel [wil] *n* rou
when [wenn] (*interr.*) kilè
whence [wenns] *adv* kidonk
whenever [wenèvèu] nenpòt kilè
where [wèr] (*interr.*) kikote
whet [wèt] *v* ile
which [witch] (*interr.*) kilès
while [wayl] *conj* pandan
whim [wim] *n* kapris
whirl [wèurl] *n* toubiyon
whisky [wiski] *n* wiski
whisper [wispèu] *v* chuichui
whistle [wistl] *n* siflèt/souflèt
white [wayt] *adj* blan
who [wou] (*interr.*) kimoun, kilès
whole [hol] *adj* antye, tout
wholly [holi] *adv* konplètman
why [way] (*interr.*) poukisa
wicked [wiked] *adj* mechan
wide [wayd] *adj* laj
widow [wido] *n* vèv
widower [widowèu] *n* vèf
wife [wayf] *n* madanm, fanm
wild [wayld] *adj* sovaj

will   [wil] *n* volonte
win   [win] *v* genyen
wind   [wind] *n* van
window   [windo] *n* fenèt
wine   [wayn] *n* diven
wink   [wink] *v* fèjedou, fèsiyo
winner   [winču] *n* gayan
winter   [winntèu] *n* livè
wipe   [wayp] *v* siye
wire   [wayèu] *n* fil elektrik, kab
wisdom   [wizdonm] *n* lasajès
wise   [wayz] *adj* saj
wish   [wich] *v* swete
wit   [wit] *n* entelijans, konprann
witch   [witch] *n* sòsyè
with   [witf] ak, avèk
withdraw   [witfdrò] *v* retire, rale soti
wither   [witèu] *v* fennen
withhold   [witfhold] *v* kenbe
within   [witfin] *adv* andedan
without   [widzawt] *adv* san, deyò
withstand   [witstennd] *v* reziste, sipòte
witness   [witnès] *n* temwen, *v* ateste, wè
wizard   [wizèud] *n* sòsye
woman   [woumann] *n* fanm, fi, madanm
wonder   [wonndèu] *n* mèvèy, *v* etone

wood   [woud] *n* bwa
wool   [woul] *n* lenn
word   [wèurd] *n* mo
work   [wèurk] *n/v* travay
worker   [wèukèu] *n* ouvriye, travayè
world   [wèurld] *n* lemonn
worm   [wèurm] *n* vè
worry   [wèuri] *n* traka, *v* trakase
worse   [wèurs] *adj* pi mal
worth   [wèurtf] *n* valè
wound   [wound] *n* blesi, *v* blese
wrap   [wrap] *v* vlope
wrestle   [wrèsl] *v* lite
wretch   [wrètch] *n* mizè
wretched   [wretched] *adj* mizerab
wring   [wring] *v* tòde, tòdye
wrinkle   [wrinkl] *n* rid
wrist   [wrist] *n* ponyèt
write   [wrayt] *v* ekri
wrong   [wrong] *adj* move, mal
wrought   [wròt] *adj* fòje

X

x-ray   [èksre] *n* radyografi
xenophobia   [zinofobya] *n* zenofobi, *adj* pè
  etranje
Xerox   [zeròks] *n* fotokopye
Xmas   [krismas] *n* nwèl
xylophone   [zaylofon] *n* zilofòn

Y

yard　[yard] *n* lakou, twa pye
yarn　[yarn] *n* fil
yawn　[yòn] *v* baye
year　[yir] *n* ane, lane
yearn　[yèurn] *v* sipliye
yeast　[yist] *n* leven
yell　[yèl] *v* rele, kriye
yellow　[yèlo] *adj* jòn
yes　[yès] *adv* wi
yesterday　[yèstèude] *n* yè
yet　[yèt] *adv* deja
yield　[yild] *v* donnen, bay
yolk　[yok] *n* jònze
you　[you] *prn* ou
young　[yong] *adj* jèn, jenn
your　[yòr] *prn* ou
yourself　[yòrsèlf] *prn* ou-menm
youth　[youtf] *n* lajenès

Z

zeal   [zil] *n* anprèsman
zero   [zero] *n* zero
zest   [zèst] *n* antren
zigzag   [zigzag] *n* zigzag, *v* zigzage
zinc   [zenk] *n* zenk
zip   [zip] *n* zip, *v* zipe
zip code   [zipkod] *n* kòd postal
zone   [zon] *n* zòn, rejyon
zoo   [zou] *n* zou
zoom   [zoum] *v* rale